PROPHETIC VOICES OF THE BIBLE

ENDLICH!
WAS MAN NICHT
GLEICH TUT, WIRD
NICHT GETAN —

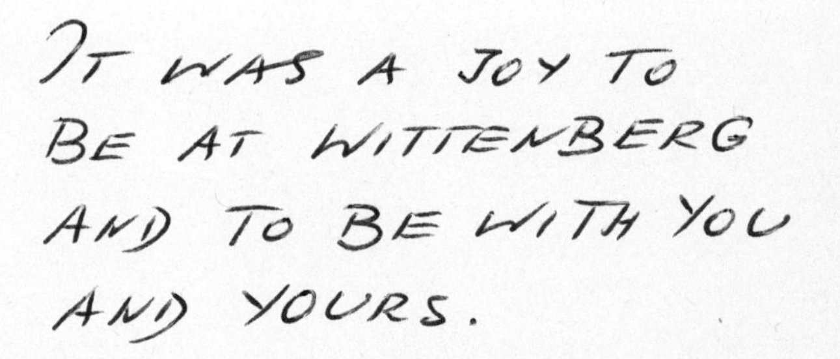

Thank you!
Hagen

PROPHETIC VOICES OF THE BIBLE

by

Hagen Staack

Hagen Staack

THIS IS A SIMPLE BOOK FOR THAT "MAN IN THE PEW" – WHICH NONE OF US WILL EVER OUT-GROW ANYHOW –

'70

THE WORLD PUBLISHING COMPANY
CLEVELAND AND NEW YORK

Published by The World Publishing Company
2231 West 110th Street, Cleveland, Ohio 44102
Published simultaneously in Canada by
Nelson, Foster & Scott Ltd.

First Printing 1968

Library of Congress Catalog Card Number: 68-26840

PRINTED IN THE UNITED STATES OF AMERICA

The artwork appearing in this book was executed for FRONTIERS OF FAITH *by NBC's Graphic Artist, Stas Pyka, and is used by permission.*

Contents

I

WHAT IS A PROPHET?

WHO are these men called prophets? Who are these strange figures appearing again and again in both the Hebrew Bible and the New Testament, interrupting the flow of the biblical story? Are they merely religious eccentrics, out of step with their own and every age, whose one-sided preaching can safely be ignored?

The prophets and their message are at the heart of biblical faith; their words are as pertinent today as in their own times. Their oddities of manner and speech should not deter us from learning who they are, what traits and message they share, and how they can still teach and lead us. To ignore them is to give up our birthright, for we are all spiritual heirs of the prophets.

When a term is overworked it can become empty; stretched to cover too much, it begins to mean very little. A prophet, as originally conceived in the Old Testament, was simply someone who spoke in the name of the Lord God. He was a man whose words were more than his own, a man through whom God spoke. The prophet was a "mouthpiece," a channel used by Almighty God to address His people and the world. This is the primary meaning of the term, around which other meanings cluster.

In our day, "prophet" suggests mainly a person who can predict the future, especially under divine guidance and inspiration. Hearing the word "prophecy," we think first of seeing the curtain drawn, the heavens opened, the future revealed, God's "letters" written somewhere; or perhaps of hearing God's voice. We may also associate the word with expressing the revelation in a weird and special language.

Applied to the Old Testament prophets, there is some aptness in this popular conception. We do associate the prophets with *visions,* a word derived from the Latin *visio:* "to see." One mark of the prophet is indeed such "seeing." He is a man not only of unusually keen perception but of a special revelation of God and the word. Sometimes, in fact, a prophet might even be called a "seer" (Amos 7:12).

The Greek language supplies us with another insight into the prophets' attributes. The word "ecstasy" stems from the Greek term meaning "to stand beside oneself." Often this is what we mean by "prophet"—a man beside himself, caught up wholly in someone or something bigger than himself.

Words like "vision" and "ecstasy" help us to understand a little better what the prophets were like but not really what they did, what their role was in ancient Israel. We have mentioned their chief function: to speak in the name of the Lord God. Again, the Greek underlying our English word "prophet" is helpful. The Greek noun *prophetēs* comes from a verb which means literally "to speak before." Here, "before" (*pro-*) means, not "in advance of" or "prior to," but "in front of" other people. To prophesy, then, originally meant "to proclaim before others, to announce in public." The prophet was called to speak in the name of the Lord to the people of the Lord. He was not a soothsayer, predicting the future, nor was he a professor of theology, expounding abstract ideas of God. He was called to speak words of judgment and hope to the people of his own generation. That required high courage, for he often had to proclaim an unpopular message. He could not trim or sweeten his message, for it came from the Lord. And because he had been called by the Lord, he had to be ready to take the consequences of speaking His word.

It takes a leap of imagination for us to see the prophets in a clear and realistic light. As we look back at their lives and writings, they appear to be heroic figures. Their names are legendary, their books immortalized, glory has been heaped upon them. Yet it is significant that each of the prophets felt his insufficiency and knew his limitations, his spiritual poverty, measured against his call. Each did what he knew he must do, but in most cases only after initial hesitation or long struggle or deep despair. The prophets' stature in our eyes should not blind us to their unpopularity in their own times, when they often met with scorn, hatred, or outright persecution. The biblical record shows also that no matter how stern and unwavering they may have seemed to their contemporaries, many of them were inwardly plagued, frustrated, disillusioned, disheartened. To understand these men and their message, we must learn to see them as humans with many of the foibles and limitations common to all men.

Yet the striking feature of the stories is how each of the prophets overcame his misgivings and carried out the Lord's assignment. "My servants, the prophets" is what the Lord calls them in the book of Jeremiah (7:25). They were true ministers in the sense of servants, entrusted with a word to carry to their people, obedient to their call whatever the cost.

Many men of the Bible were called prophets in their own time; many more have been so named by later generations. To look at a few of the great personalities of the early periods may help us to discern the marks of the prophet and the prophetic spirit.

Who was the first of the prophets? Abraham? Moses? Joshua? Samuel? In the Old Testament (Genesis 12:2) as well as in the New Testament (Matthew 1:1; John 8:39), Abraham is called the father of the Hebrew people. In a sense one might also call him the father of the prophets and even the first of the prophets. Although the Scriptures never apply the name to him, he exhibits many of the characteristics of the prophet. He was specially called by the Lord (Genesis 12:1 ff.), and his obedience to the call meant leaving behind a settled, secure existence for a future whose only certainty was God's word of promise. He proclaimed God Almighty (Genesis 17:1), "maker of heaven and earth" (14:22), in the pagan world surrounding him. The prophetic spirit seems as old as the people which traces its roots back to Abraham.

The commanding figure of Moses adds other dimensions to this prophetic tradition. He was the leader in the exodus from Egypt, the central event in the making of a real nation, Israel, out of a conglomerate of peoples. With the exodus, Israel stepped from obscurity into history, and it was Moses who, under God, led them there. That is one mark of the Old Testament prophets: they were involved in the politics of their day, in the making of history. At least to this degree, Moses, although he is not listed among the prophets in the table of contents of our Bibles, could be called a prophet. A postscript to the book of Deuteronomy, describing the death of Moses, does just that: "And there has not arisen a prophet since in Israel like Moses, whom the Lord knew face to face" (Deuteronomy 34:10).

One clear mark of the prophet is that each knew the Lord in some special, direct, and immediate fashion. Moses was singled out and confronted by the Lord in the appearance at the burning bush (Exodus 3). The later prophets had similar experiences of being set apart and met directly: Isaiah saw the Lord seated on a throne in the temple, resplendent and terrible in His holiness (Isaiah 6). To Ezekiel, He appeared on a throne mounted on the wheels of a chariot (Ezekiel 1). Jeremiah was told that the Lord had known him and set him apart to be a prophet while he was still in his mother's womb (Jeremiah 1).

Moses' experience on Mount Sinai (Horeb) is crucial for understanding the prophets. There, alone with God, he was given the rules of the covenant between the Lord and the people He had liberated from slavery in Egypt (Exodus 20). To this covenant in the wilderness all later prophets harked back, for it defined the people's special mission from God, the rules for their faithfulness and obedience to Him, and the sense of oneness under the Lord that defined them as a people. Sometimes the prophets sound monotonous in their recall of the covenant, for the people drifted away from it and paid the prophets little heed.

Moses fits the prophetic pattern for yet another reason. He encountered indifference and fickleness at the very beginning of Israel's nationhood. When he came down from the mountain he found the people dancing around a golden calf, to which they were ascribing their deliverance from slavery. Moses, in a burst of anger, then shattered the tables of stone. His action expressed a zeal typical of most of the prophets of Israel. They were animated by a passion for the Lord and His covenant, which often burst forth in righteous wrath and indignation.

What about Joshua, the next great figure to appear on the stage of Israel's history? As a military commander, Joshua's brilliant strategy conquered the land of Canaan in order that the tribes of Israel could settle it. His achievements laid the groundwork for the future kingdoms of David and Solomon.

Yet Joshua is never called a prophet anywhere in the Scriptures. If we pause to study him, therefore, it might help us better to establish the profile of the prophet.

Like the prophets, Joshua received instructions from the Lord, but he translated these into action, into leadership in battle and conquest. The prophets frequently advised military commanders and rulers, but they themselves usually did not lead into battle or hold in their hands the reins of government. Even if Moses is regarded as an exception to this rule, yet the rule prevailed through the remainder of Israel's history. It is against the foil of those who did rule in Israel that one sees most clearly the prophetic profile. For one function of the prophet was to see that the king, as well as the people, did not violate the covenant. To do so, the prophet had to remain detached from political maneuvers, however "involved in politics" he might be from the standpoint of a critic and an interpreter of the covenant faith. Thus Israelite prophecy came to its fullest flower under the Israelite monarchy.

There is another difference between Joshua and the prophets. In his finest hour, when he renewed the Lord's covenant with Israel and made them promise to be faithful, Joshua was a great religious as well as a national leader. But something was missing. "Now, therefore," he tells the people gathered at Shechem, "fear the Lord, and serve him in sincerity and faithfulness; put away the gods which your father served beyond the river, and in Egypt, and serve the Lord." But he does not fervently denounce the people. "If you be unwilling to serve the Lord," he says, "choose this day whom you will serve . . . but as for me and my house, we will serve the Lord" (Joshua 24:14–15). There is personal decision and clarity in this approach, but the inspiring fervor of the prophets is missing. The spiritual authority of one who speaks in the name of the Lord is absent. The true prophet resembles lightning streaking to earth out of darkness, bringing light to a chaotic world. His impact is as the eruption of the awakened volcano. He cannot be ignored. He is the voice crying in the wilderness, proclaiming a new highway on which God may come to dwell among His people.

After the death of Joshua and his generation, Israel entered into a dark phase of its history, the period of the judges. In these two centuries Israel was preserved, in spite of disunity and disloyalty, by men and women who rose up to lead in moments of threat and crisis. Their military exploits in guiding the Israelite tribes to victory against their hostile neighbors are recounted in the book of Judges. Some of these judges revealed authentic elements of the prophet. When Israel was threatened with dissolution and its faith with extinction, the judges united the people around their Lord. In looking back at the period of the judges, Israel learned from it that while their unfaithfulness to the Lord led to judgment, His judgment was intended not for their destruction but for their deliverance. Israel would later experience this grace of God in a new way when, before sending destruction, the Lord sent His messengers, the prophets, to warn of the coming judgment.

The last of the judges, Samuel, was a prophet in the *full sense of the word.* Even as a young boy he had the sense of being singled out by God for a personal mission. When he heard God calling him, the old priest Eli heard nothing. His loneliness as a prophet continued throughout his life, for he had to proclaim what God revealed to a people who would rather have done without his message. All his life Samuel bore this burden. Even in the grave the prophetic spirit was not left in peace! The first book of Samuel tells of a time when a desperate King Saul forced a medium to call back Samuel's spirit, which, in the prophetic tradition, delivered a dire prophecy to the king: "Because you did not obey the voice of the Lord, and did not carry out his fierce wrath against Amalek, therefore the Lord has done this thing to you this day. Moreover the Lord will give Israel also with you into the hand of the Philistines; and tomorrow you and your sons shall be with me; the Lord will give the army of Israel also into the hand of the Philistines" (I Samuel 28:18–19). Samuel is the outstanding example of the prophet who never shirked his calling, even when his message was unpopular and his hearers ignored his counsel.

The importance of the prophet as God's spokesman stands out clearly in the career of Nathan. Officially appointed as a prophet in the court of King David, Nathan was the spiritual guardian not only over the king but over all Israel-Judah. When David had taken Bathsheba to be his wife, after issuing the order that resulted in the death of her husband, Uriah, Nathan dared to stand before the king and denounce his deed. He could face Israel's greatest leader and tell David to his face that he had violated God's covenant in doing such a terrible thing to a good and loyal subject. Nathan then pronounced a severe judgment on David's dynasty, a punishment which would be meted out to his children and his children's children. King David did not exile or imprison the prophet, as any other oriental ruler would have done. He listened to the prophetic voice and bowed himself in repentance before his God (II Samuel 11–12). The scene dramatizes the Bible's sense that the prophets speak in the name of a God from whose judgments *no one* is immune. Such heroism on the part of prophets sometimes makes them seem to be men without fear, a group of supermen. As we have seen and will see again, they are really men of flesh and blood, like ourselves; but their fear of men is superseded by their much greater fear of God.

The profile of the prophet becomes clearer when we see it in relation to another group of religious leaders, the priests. After David had taken the stronghold of Jerusalem and made it his capital, the temple was established and the priesthood began to grow in power. The priest had always occupied a favored position in Israel. In the accounts of Israel's wilderness wanderings, Aaron is often depicted standing by Moses' side (for example, Exodus 7–8). These accounts speak of him as "the priest" (Exodus 31:10) and the founder of the priesthood (Exodus 29:1–9). At first, Israel had many places of sacrifice and worship. We see Samuel officiating now at

Ramah (I Samuel 9), now at Gilgal (I Samuel 10:8). Later, however, all worship was concentrated in the temple in Jerusalem, both because of the prestige attached to the temple and because the outlying shrines were subject to corruption from the Canaanite paganism then prevailing in the towns and countryside. These shrines gradually declined in importance, and the Jerusalem priests grew more powerful. They became involved in political maneuvers, and the future of the empire sometimes seemed to depend on them.

In character and function the priest was a conservative person. He insisted on maintaining the established traditions of the fathers and regarded worship as right and proper only when it was done as it had always been done. The society accorded the priest his place of honor, and the priest, in turn, would try to maintain the society. If the temple was well kept, and if the leading citizens supported the priesthood, why should the priests not reciprocate by backing the social *status quo?* The alliance between the priestly altar and the royal throne also seemed natural, one of mutual glorification and mutual assistance.

There is no doubt that this conservative element is a part of any religion. In a world where the only certainty is the inevitability of changes, it is good to have something tried and tested to hold on to. As the song expresses it, if "that old-time religion" was good enough for grandfather and grandmother, father and mother and brother, "it's good enough for me." But religion in this sense can become largely a heritage from the past, to which one clings, and which offers some false sense of strength and support in a continually changing world.

This is the point at which the great prophets of Israel enter the picture. As we have seen, they too look back repeatedly to Israel's heritage from those days in the wilderness when the Lord made a covenant with his chosen people. But the faces of the prophets are not averted from the present or the future, as if all good lay in the past or were enshrined in ancient traditions. This was because for them God was not a God only of the past, of Moses and his generation. Untiringly they pointed out that adherence to the covenant inherited from the past must show itself in changed behavior in the present, or dire consequences would follow in the future.

This sense of "God here and now" is the basis of the prophets' attack upon the traditional forms of worship and sacrifice in their day. If these forms fostered a kind of stand-still religion that drowned men's spirit in tradition, lulling their consciences and suffocating their sense of justice, then the prophets cried out against it. Even if they were or had been priests themselves (like Ezekiel) they felt compelled to say that God did not really want sacrifices, elaborate temples, ornate altars, or a host of bejeweled and bedecked priests. If burnt offerings, incense, and solemn assemblies were only empty, routinized manifestations of an *ersatz* faith diluted from the substance of true faith in the Lord, then the Lord hated and despised them all (Amos 5:21–24). How could men offer sacrifices with hands stained with the blood of their brothers in the covenant (Isaiah 1)? What the Lord wanted, said the prophets, was that men should "do justice and love kindness" (Micah 6:8). "Let justice roll down like waters, and righteousness like an ever-flowing stream" (Amos 5:24). The prophets spoke out against the established religion of their day because, for them, religion went deep and was not bound to a special time or place: it was a continuing lifetime commitment.

Although the prophets were not afraid to pronounce harsh words of punishment, all of them knew the word of grace and of love. "They are messengers of God's wrath," one scholar has noted, "but it is due to his merciful goodness that instead of judgment itself, the messengers of judgment came." When we read the prophets' pronouncements of doom in the following chapters, we should always bear in mind that God's grace underlies His messages of wrath. He seeks only that men may turn from their evil ways and live.

For the Christian, Jesus Christ seems to sum up and reveal what the prophets said and stood for. "For the Christian, it is impossible to understand Jesus Christ without seeing him as both the heir and the re-creator of the prophetic movement. He seems to sum up the great themes and work of the prophets. In him we find the same lonely sense of calling to a divine mis-

"YAHWEH is God." This strong declaration is a literal translation of the name Elijah. From the dramatic stories in I Kings 17, 18, 19, and 21* there emerges a strong personality whose name is a motto for his life, indeed a battle cry: "Yahweh is God!"

Chapter 16 of I Kings tells us about the political situation in Judah and Israel, the two kingdoms that resulted when the glorious kingdom of David and Solomon divided *ca.* 922 B.C. A comparison of the two kingdoms shows that the political situation in the southern kingdom, Judah, was relatively stable. There was only one dynasty, the house of David, and one king followed another in orderly succession. Israel, however, was filled with unrest, plagued by frequent changes in the sequence of kings and ruling dynasties. One king, Zimri, ruled only seven days (I Kings 16:15). Because the political situation was unstable, there was general insecurity and restiveness among the people.

Around the year 869 B.C. a man named Ahab was elevated to the throne of Israel, succeeding his father Omri, a great military commander who had led the successful revolt against Zimri and then seized the throne (I Kings 16:15–22). The Elijah stories paint a dismal picture of Ahab. From them we get the impression that he had totally succumbed to foreign religious fertility cults and all sorts of superstitious activities. Yet, other clues in the Bible indicate that he had not completely rejected Yahweh as the God of Israel. For example, the names he gave his children bear the sacred syllable that appears in Elijah's name. And in the latter part of Ahab's reign, we are told that

* Most of what we know about Elijah is contained in these four chapters; in addition there are a few verses about him in the first chapter of II Kings. The Greek version of the Old Testament, the Septuagint (LXX), places chapter 21 directly after chapter 19, indicating that (in the second century B.C. and earlier) these four chapters were thought to belong together. The same conclusion is suggested by the style of the Elijah stories, which is different from that of the surrounding chapters.

he consulted the prophets of Yahweh. It seems, therefore, that Ahab was just tolerant and what we would call "eclectic." (II Kings 10:18 says he "served Baal a little.") He did not worship the Lord exclusively, nor did he completely reject Him. Elijah objected to Ahab's easygoing tolerance and not only preached but actively worked against the king.

We can understand Elijah's deep hostility only if we turn to Ahab's wife, the infamous Queen Jezebel. It was her powerful influence and intrigue that Elijah probably saw as the chief threat to Israel and to the worship of Yahweh.

Jezebel, attractive and clever, was born to be a queen. As the daughter of Eth-Baal, the king of the Phoenician city of Sidon (I Kings 16:31), her marriage to Ahab sealed an alliance with Phoenicia, then at the height of its power. When Jezebel came to the court of Israel, she brought with her the gods of her homeland, Baal and Asherah. It seems likely that Ahab, a courageous warrior and good general (he once defeated a Syrian army much larger than his own forces), was anxious to keep peace at home and to preserve the alliance. To give in to Jezebel on religious matters was the easier course, and Ahab took it. He even built a temple for Baal in Samaria (I Kings 16:32).

We can see that it would be an extremely delicate thing—upsetting to the political order, and worth a man's life—to protest openly the introduction of these foreign gods. But that is just what Elijah did. And that is just why Ahab called him "you troubler of Israel" (I Kings 18:17). As we shall see in a later chapter (pp. 33–34) the Baal cult and its fertility rites were not new in Israel. It was the religion of the land before the Israelites entered in conquest, and it continued as a serious rival to the worship of the Lord for a long time after the Israelites had settled there. With Jezebel, however, the worship of Baal entered Israel bearing the prestige of a mighty god of a successful, sophisticated, and powerful people—and an ally at that. Moreover, Jezebel had the power of the throne behind her efforts to impose Baal worship on the Israelites, for she knew how to handle her husband and the political notables in Israel.

The story of Naboth and his vineyard tells us a great deal about Jezebel's attitude and how she worked. As the story is told in I Kings 21, it is a lesson in the art of how to succeed in queenship without obviously breaking the "rules." Naboth owned a vineyard which the king wanted. Ahab told Naboth he would give him a better vineyard in exchange for it or pay him what it was worth in money (21:2). But the vineyard had been in the family a long time, and Naboth did not want to part with it. Accustomed to the rather democratic ways of Israel, he refused, and the king, used to the same democratic traditions, gave up, went home, and pouted: "And he lay down on his bed, and turned away his face, and would eat no food" (21:4). At this point Jezebel took command. She came from a land where the king's word was law and his wishes or whims were satisfied without question. She could not understand or tolerate a state of affairs where a mere subject could refuse the king. "Do you now govern Israel?" she asked her husband. "Arise, and eat bread, and let your heart be cheerful; I will give you the vineyard of Naboth the Jezreelite" (21:7).

Jezebel could get the vineyard for nothing only if Naboth's property could be made forfeit to the king: Naboth must be found guilty of blaspheming God and dishonoring the king (21:10). As this could be accomplished only by devious means, Jezebel had to find accomplices among the Israelites, who would themselves be involved in the crime and so be unable to accuse her without implicating themselves. In Ahab's name she wrote letters to the elders and nobles in the city where Naboth lived, asking them to prefer false charges against Naboth that would discredit him, lead to his stoning, and make his property forfeit. All cooperated very nicely. For the collaborators it probably meant the removal of a competitor. The price they paid was that Jezebel now had a hold on them. The plan worked perfectly: the queen had the vineyard, she had new allies, and she had Naboth out of the picture (or thought she had).

But the Lord's covenant with His people did not allow such dealings, even on the part of a king—or a queen. The next scene shows us Elijah confronting Ahab in Naboth's vineyard.

If Ahab, coming to claim his property, had thought he was really getting away with something, he was now brought up short by the question from the Lord, spoken by Elijah: "Have you killed, and also taken possession?" (21:19). "Thus says the Lord: 'In the place where dogs licked up the blood of Naboth shall dogs lick your own blood' " (21:19). Elijah then pronounced doom on Jezebel and the whole house of Ahab: " 'The dogs shall eat Jezebel within the bounds of Jezreel.' Any one belonging to Ahab who dies in the city, the dogs shall eat; and any one of his who dies in the open country the birds of the air shall eat" (21:23–24). This punishment sounds ruthless, and it was. To understand Elijah's severity, we must remember that at this point he was protesting far more than the ruler's "religious tolerance." He was incensed by the extreme cruelty to Naboth. Who would defend Naboth's cause, and the cause of the poor and the oppressed, in a land where there was no Supreme Court to decide between ruler and people? Elijah sees what is right and just, and he speaks bluntly, without compromise or tolerance. This concern for justice and for the cause of those who cannot defend themselves is a major theme that is repeated throughout the prophetic tradition. Hard times call for hard words, and Elijah and the prophets that follow are called to speak them. If this led them to pronounce harsh judgment, they did so because of their total conviction and faithfulness to Yahweh.

The clearest example of this severity is the great scene on Mount Carmel, the mountain range that marks the southern border of the plain of Jezreel. All mountains in Palestine run from north to south, except the Mount Carmel range, which cuts across from east to west. This natural barrier had become very important during Solomon's time, and the fortifications he built at Megiddo still guarded this northern gate to the Hebrew territories.

Even today one can see numerous caves in the limestone formations of the Mount Carmel range. Native guides claim they can show *the* cave in which Elijah *hid from Ahab* during the great drought, as well as other caves where, presumably, other persecuted prophets found refuge (I Kings 18:4).

Whatever his hiding place, Elijah emerged from it to announce a great contest. That Ahab was still somehow faithful to Yahweh alongside the other gods he tolerated is shown by the fact that he listened to the Lord's prophet and carried out Elijah's orders for setting up the contest (I Kings 18:19). With the sweeping claim that he was the sole remaining servant of the Lord in Israel (18:22)—an overstatement, as we shall see later—the prophet challenged the priests of Baal and Asherah to gather at Mount Carmel for the contest (18:23–24). What Elijah was challenging was the Israelites' belief that there was more than one god, and that they could serve more than one god: "How long will you go limping with two different opinions? If the Lord is God, follow him" (18:21).

Two altars were set up. Two bulls were then prepared for sacrifice and placed on the wood. The wood on the altars was not to be lighted. Instead, the prophets were to pray to their respective deities, who would ignite the wood and consume the sacrifice.

The narrative, beginning in I Kings 18:20, has something of the carnival atmosphere of a big circus. Here was the lone prophet Elijah pitted against 450 pagan priests. The stakes were the highest: to make clear once and for all who the real God was, Baal or Yahweh; who was his representative; and who could rightfully claim the allegiance of a whole nation. We are told that the priests of Baal danced a ritual dance, and slapped themselves with swords and lances until they were covered with their own blood (18:28). Elijah seemed to enjoy their complete lack of success. "Cry aloud" to Baal, he taunts them, "for he is a god; either he is musing, or he has gone aside, or he is on a journey, or perhaps he is asleep and must be awakened" (18:27).

When the priests of Baal were exhausted, Elijah began. Elijah was a great showman and made the most of his unusual opportunity. His altar was built up high, "in the name of the Lord" (18:32). He dug a trench around it, filled the trench with water, and even drenched the altar and the sacrifice to make the igniting of the pyre more difficult (18:33–35). Elijah then prayed to the Lord, and "the fire of the Lord fell, and consumed the burnt offering, and the wood, and the stones, and the dust, and licked up the water that was in the trench" (18:38). The Israelites assembled on Mount Carmel could see that the Baal whom the priests had called upon either did not exist or was powerless. Falling on their faces, the Israelites confessed, "The Lord, he is God; the Lord, he is God" (18:39). The prophets of Baal were brought down to the foot of the mountain and killed.

Now that it was clear who was God in Israel, it would also be made clear that He, and not Baal, gave rain and fertility. Elijah instructed his servant, "Go up, say to Ahab, 'Prepare your chariot and go down, lest the rain stop you' " (18:44). After a drought extending over three years, the land was revived by a drenching rain.

Elijah's dramatic victory on Mount Carmel is indeed impressive. At the same time it disturbs us to read about all those priests killed at the edge of the Brook Kishon. There is no doubt that this was cruelty without a trace of love, without the smallest sign of willingness to help others see the truth and find the way. Elijah could not compromise. Those of us who may find it easy to judge Elijah, however, and to point out his faults, might ask ourselves whether we have ever been locked in a life-and-death struggle for what we hold most dear, and what our actions would have been under those circumstances. Or have we, perhaps, never felt strongly enough about anything to take a determined stand? Elijah did, and because of it he had to run for his life.

After the slaughter of the Baal prophets had been reported to Jezebel, she "sent a messenger to Elijah, saying, 'So may the gods do to me and more also, if I do not make your life as the life of one of them by this time tomorrow' " (I Kings 19:2). Now the "troubler of Israel" had cause to be troubled himself. He fled south through Israel and most of the territory of Judah. Leaving his servant in Beersheba, on the edge of the Judean desert, the Negev, he continued on his way "a day's journey into the wilderness" (19:3–4). He was desperate, and not merely, perhaps, because of the threat to his life. True, it seemed that God had put His seal of approval on Elijah's work, but what had Elijah really accomplished? He had had to flee at the moment of success; and now, after the long journey, he seemed weary of life itself. Under a broom tree he sat down and talked to God. "It is enough; now, O Lord, take away my life; for I am no better than my fathers" (19:4).

After this outcry of despair, Elijah slept. When he awoke and had eaten and drunk, the angel of the Lord led him ever southward, until, after walking forty days and forty nights, he arrived at Mount Horeb (Sinai), the sacred mountain of God (19:8). We remember that this is the hallowed place where Hebrew tradition said that Moses had received the law, and where the Hebrew people had entered into covenant with the Lord and become a nation. It is also the setting of the narrative telling about the time Moses was permitted to see the train of the garment of God (Exodus 33:17–23).

Elijah, too, was led to a cave on the mountain, and was confronted there by the Lord. "What are you doing here, Elijah?" asked the Lord (I Kings 19:9). And Elijah replied, "I have been very jealous for the Lord, the God of hosts; for the people of Israel have forsaken thy covenant, thrown down thy altars, and slain thy prophets with the sword; and I, even I only, am left; and they seek my life, to take it away" (19:10).

Elijah made two mistakes. First, he gave himself a little too much credit; and second, he assumed that he was the only faithful adherent of the true religion.

Elijah learned. Up there alone on the mountain before the Lord, he waited for the Lord to make himself known. There was a violent storm, then an earthquake, then a fire, but the Lord was in none of these (19:11–12). After the fire, there came "a still small voice" (19:12), and Elijah hid his face in his mantle because it is not man's right to see God. He stepped outside and stood at the entrance of the cave. Again the voice asked, "What are you doing here, Elijah?" and Elijah again replied, "I have been very jealous for the Lord, the God of hosts; for the people of Israel have forsaken thy covenant, thrown down thy altars, and slain thy prophets with the sword, and I, even I only, am left; and they seek my life, to take it away" (19:13–14). This incident surely made Elijah aware of the contrast between his own melodramatic claims and the presence of the Lord, who did not speak out of storm, earthquake, or fire, but in the still, small voice.

The next words the Lord spoke to Elijah began with, "Go, return . . ." (19:15). Elijah's wish for a quick end in the wilderness was not granted. His weariness of life is countered with a new commission: his life is worth living because the Lord still has work for him to do. He was sent, not to Israel, however, but to Damascus, to anoint a new king over Syria (19:15). The foreigner would become an instrument of the God who is active in all history. Only then would Elijah be permitted to anoint as king over Israel a man who would rectify Ahab's wrongs (19:16). And only then would he be permitted to anoint his successor in the prophetic office, Elisha, the son of Shaphat (19:16). The battle for the true faith was not over, but it was thus placed into a larger context and lost its taste of personal success and personal glory for Elijah.

Elijah was also told that he was not really so isolated as he had thought. The Lord said He still had seven thousand in Israel, "all the knees that have not bowed to Baal, and every mouth that has not kissed him" (19:18). It must have been a jolt for Elijah to be told that he was not the only one, and that there were seven thousand faithful. In Hebrew usage this did not mean literally and exactly seven thousand. "Seven" was a sacred number, the sacred number of the quarter of the moon, the sacred number of the days of the week, while "thousands" was understood to represent an uncountable number. Elijah was being informed that there were quite a few, and that he, Elijah, should come down from his mountain of self-imposed loneliness.

It seems difficult for us to recognize that God's faithful are known only to Himself. We are warned by what happened to Elijah that God has more true servants than many like to believe, and in places where we might least expect to find them. It is hard for a strong leader to see himself as only one among many children of the Lord: the tendency is to equate his own strong will with the will of God.

The end of Elijah's life came, according to biblical text, in a fashion quite different from his desire or expectation. He departed in a blaze of glory, taken up into the heavens in a "chariot of fire and horses of fire . . . and Elijah went up by a whirlwind into heaven" (II Kings 2:11). In explaining this text some writers have made it sound as though a space ship descended to take Elijah to another world. The biblical text does not require such fanciful embellishment. It is telling us that Elijah got what he had requested earlier when he asked to depart this life, although the fulfillment was different from his expressed wish. Again there is a similarity with Moses, because he, too, was taken away so that "no man knows the place of his burial to this day" (Deuteronomy 34:6). Elijah left this world in circumstances befitting his flair for showmanship, but, as with Moses, there was no shrine containing the holy man's remains, to which a pilgrimage could be made. When a man's work is done, it is God's glory only that remains.

In the New Testament only Moses, Abraham, and David are mentioned more frequently than Elijah. In the transfiguration scene on the mountain he appears with Moses, talking with Jesus (Matthew 17:1 ff.). Afterward, when Jesus' disciples asked, " 'Why do the scribes say that first Elijah must come?' Jesus replied, 'Elijah does come, and he is to restore all things; but I tell you that Elijah has already come, and they did not know him, but did to him whatever they pleased. So also the Son of Man will suffer at their hands.' Then the disciples understood that he was speaking to them of John the Baptist" (17:10–13). Moses and Elijah were thought of by Jesus and His contemporaries as key persons in the coming of the Messianic age. How frail, how imperfect, how human were these two great men. Yet God was able to use them for His purposes. The mantle of prophecy passed from Elijah to Elisha, through the prophets we shall look at in succeeding chapters, to John the Baptist. It is an absorbing story, filled with surprises, and we shall now pursue it further.

III

AMOS

THE AGITATOR FROM THE SOUTH

And the Lord said, "Amos, what do you see? . . . Behold, I am setting a plumbline in the midst of my people Israel."

IN our time we always look for "firsts"—the first man to enter space or reach the moon, to run a four-minute mile, to cure cancer. Amos must be credited with scoring several firsts. So far as we know, he is the first prophet to commit his utterances to writing. As we have seen, there were prophets before, such as Samuel, Nathan, Elijah, and his successor, Elisha. There were even groups or "bands" of prophets (I Samuel 10:5) in Israel and Judah. But Amos was the first whose words were recorded in a separate book bearing his name.

The language of the book of Amos is direct and straight to the point, like Amos himself. He was a rough-hewn man who did not stand on ceremony. Today we might say that he had no sense of "public relations." He did not sugarcoat his words to make them palatable. But what he said struck home.

We know few details of the life and personality of Amos. Tekoa, the village he gives as his home town, was a small place a few miles south of Jerusalem. We know that, at the time, Uzziah ruled in Judah and Jeroboam II in Israel. All evidence considered, we can place Amos near the year 750 B.C.

Although one can infer many things about Amos from a careful reading of his book, the only explicit information is given in the first verse of chapter 1 and in chapter 7, where he encounters Amaziah, the ruling priest of the royal sanctuary of Beth-El. Amaziah expected Amos to be one of the run-of-the-mill professionals who made a good living with their so-called prophesying. We are given some indication of this kind of "prophesying" in the books of Samuel, where it is said that "he who is now called a prophet was formerly called a seer" (I Samuel 9:9), that is, one gifted with special powers enabling him to predict the future. That was, and is today, a common image of a prophet: someone who foresees the future. In Amos' day, and even earlier, there were many such seers or foretellers who advised or warned others about the future and were often paid well for their services. Astrology, an established art among the Babylonians, was a common property of all peoples of the Fertile Crescent.

Amos violently denied that he was a "prophet" in this popular sense. He wanted no part of such prophets and refused to be recognized as such by his people.

> "I am no prophet, nor a prophet's son; but I am a herdsman, and a dresser of sycamore tress, and the Lord took me from following the flock, and the Lord said to me, 'Go, prophesy to my people Israel.' "
>
> AMOS 7:14–15

It took courage for Amos to appear with his message at Beth-El, Israel's national sanctuary, where he probably began his preaching. It required greater courage to preach in or at Samaria, the capital city of the Northern Kingdom, where he took his message later. The fearless man with an unpopular message could hardly expect to make money prophesying. Instead, he could look forward to indignant reactions and persecution—and that was his reward. In a double sense, Amos was what his name means in Hebrew, a "burden-bearer." He bore the burden of a heavy message from the Lord, and bore the burden of an Israel that had forgotten its Lord and forsaken His covenant. For Amos was not one who sat on the throne of the just, pointing a righteous finger at others. As we listen to him preaching we can hear how pained he was by the things he had to say, because Israel was his own flesh and blood, and he was part of the same covenant. This is the clue to the story of Amos. In spite of the division of the Hebrews into two kingdoms, in spite of their "whoring after foreign gods" and their callous disregard of social justice, Amos felt deeply that his people were the people of the one covenant God.

This is why Amos felt compelled to leave the bleak countryside where he made a living by herding sheep and goats. His was a lonely life enlivened only by encounters with wild animals (Amos 3:12) or by an occasional walk with another human—by appointment! (3:3). Amos also speaks of himself as "a dresser of sycamore trees" (7:14). The sycamore produces a fruit similar to the fig, which is often attacked by insects that burrow deep inside. To save even a part of the fruit for harvesting, it had to be punctured by hand to release the insects. With this work Amos supplemented his income from tending his stock.

This, then, was no urban sophisticate who came to speak in polished phrases in the busy, prosperous towns and cities of Israel. Rather, here was a man accustomed to hard work and the lonely life, yet so moved by his concern for Israel that he left the quiet security of his southern homeland to venture north to preach.

At first, the people in Beth-El liked the rustic herdsman from Tekoa who spoke so knowingly in their town. He began by denouncing Damascus, saying that a fire would devour its strongholds and the Syrians would go into exile. This forecast of doom for a traditional enemy was discerning and praiseworthy. They encouraged Amos to go on. So he talked about the Philistine city of Gaza, and predicted that fire would fall upon them. One by one, Amos named the great cities of the Philistines that were set apart for destruction. Again, the listeners told Amos to continue. Then came Tyre and Edom, and Ammon and Moab, and his hearers grew excited. This prophecy took care of all the enemies, showing that their evil ways would bring about their well-deserved downfall.

So far, what Amos was saying was nothing new. In the utterance recorded in chapter 2:9 ff., he recalls how the Amorites were once hewn down like so many cedars before the advancing columns of the Hebrews as they emerged from the wilderness. He speaks of Egypt as the land of slavery from which the Lord had once liberated Israel. In saying that God is the God who acts and works among all nations and all peoples to achieve His ends, Amos was following a time-honored Hebrew tradition.

Having gained the attention and support of his hearers in Beth-El, Amos drew the net even closer to home. He proceeded to tell them about the punishment to be meted out to Judah, Israel's sister kingdom to the south. "I will send a fire upon Judah and it shall devour the strongholds of Jerusalem" (Amos 2:5). Even this met with the approval of the people of Beth-El, because to them the southerners were traitors to the nation and the faith. They were the secessionists. Were they the ones to choose their own king, to claim for themselves Jerusalem, the city chosen by David as the capital for *all* the Hebrews? Surely they deserved to get their comeuppance!

But what was this country bumpkin shouting now? "For three transgressions of Israel and for four," Amos went on, "I will not revoke the punishment; because they sell the righteous for silver, and the needy for a pair of shoes—they that trample the head of the poor into the dust of the earth and turn aside the way of the afflicted" (2:6, 7). "You made the Nazirites drink wine," he continued, "and commanded the prophets, saying, 'You shall not prophesy' " (2:12).

Was he talking about Israel? About *us?* Here the people of Beth-El drew the line. It had always been a temptation for the Israelites, the "chosen people," to fashion from their history a special and permanent place in the sun, to believe that God protects His own, come what may. This leads easily to saying it is God's *duty* to take care of His favorites—the "good guys."

This temptation comes to every man and nation. On the evening that Sputnik was sent into orbit, a prominent man in an American community asked how God could allow the godless Russians to get ahead of Christian Americans. Why did God not see to it that "His own" occupied first place in the world? This was the reaction Amos encountered when he began to make his real point.

It was all right to have prophets around, but not one who announced punishment and doom for the Lord's own people. When all was going well and everyone (almost everyone) was enjoying high living standards, what call had this agitator from the south to stick his nose in where it did not belong? Who did Amos think he was? Was this not Beth-El, "the house of God," where the Lord had spoken to Jacob (Genesis 35:15) and where the king had his sanctuary?

But Amos went on with his catalogue of Israel's sins, proclaiming the Lord's judgment despite the loud protests of his audience. Finally the priest Amaziah stepped in and got rid of Amos with the words, "O seer, go, flee away to the land of Judah, and eat bread there, and prophesy there; but never again prophesy at Bethel, for it is the king's sanctuary, and it is a temple of the kingdom" (Amos 7:12). Here the chief priest directed all the authority of church and state against one lonely herdsman.

Amos knew he was a layman, neither a priest nor a recognized prophet nor a prophet's son. But when these professionals failed to speak out in the name of the Lord, he, a shepherd and laborer, felt compelled to speak. He knew he was on sure ground, for the call he had heard and the message he announced were within the tradition of Moses and other champions of the Lord. He turned to God's past dealings, citing Sodom and Gomorrah as examples (4:11) and mentioning persons and events from the history of Israel. Amos had walked where others had been before him, and he spoke not from selfish concern, but as the burden-bearer of the Lord.

What were Amos' reasons for speaking as he did, first to the people of Beth-El and then to those in Samaria? What convictions lay behind his words? There are three outstanding elements in his preaching; all of them became significant in later prophetic proclamation.

The first is that Israel's faith must manifest itself in concern for the poor, for the underdog, for the suffering, for those at the bottom of the social ladder. Amos insisted, as did later prophets, that the quality of social justice is the gauge of righteousness in a people. To express concern for those who have less and suffer more, who do not have the strength themselves to climb to higher levels—this usually thankless job of social justice is one of God's measures of a nation.

One can hardly ascribe to Amos grand social schemes outlining comprehensive social service organizations to care for the poor and the destitute. Of these he knew nothing. What he wanted to see was each individual, each person in the nation, caring for his brother, for his neighbor. Today we might say that what Amos looked for and did not find in Israel was the simple willingness to bother about the next fellow.

In this context, Amos had some cutting remarks to make about some of the leading ladies of Israel. "Cows of Bashan" he called them (4:1). "Bring, that we may drink," they call to their husbands at the eighth-century B.C. equivalent of the cocktail party. Amos holds these queens of society up to the public gaze, not because he advocated abstinence or because he was a teetotaler, but because he wanted it known that these painted "cows of Bashan" had nothing better to do than push their husbands into grasping for more money, more finery, more wine—even at the expense of the poor (4:1)—so their own emptiness of soul might be filled with material goods.

The second element in Amos' preaching was the insistence on true and genuine worship.

> I hate, I despise your feasts,
> and I take no delight in your solemn assemblies.
> Even though you offer me your burnt offerings and
> cereal offerings,
> I will not accept them,
> and the peace offerings of your fatted beasts
> I will not look upon.
> Take away from me the noise of your songs;
> to the melody of your harps I will not listen.
> But let justice roll down like waters,
> and righteousness like an ever-flowing stream.
>
> AMOS 5:21–24

This man from the eighth century B.C. is frighteningly modern, as contemporary as the calendar before you. Amos' complaint was not that the Israelites had too little religion. He complained that they had too much. They had feast days and great assemblies galore, with all their clamor and gaudiness. There was great activity in the religious life of Israel. But it was like the "noisy gong" and the "clanging cymbal" of which St. Paul spoke centuries later (I Corinthians 13:1).

Amos scored another "first" here. With unmistakable clarity and outspokenness he showed that "religion" can be a smokescreen whereby man can obscure God and avoid serving Him. Amos pressed the point that religion could be the arch enemy of genuine faith.

Is it any wonder that the priest of Beth-El did not like him, and invoked the help of the political powers (Jeroboam, the king of Israel) to throw out this "foreigner from the south" who dared to agitate among the people of the north? For the priest Amaziah, it was no longer a question of whether Amos was right or wrong. This outsider threatened not only the prosperity of the rich but the whole framework of religious practice. And it was disconcerting to hear a pronouncement like, "Behold, I am setting a plumb line in the midst of my people Israel; I will never again pass by them" (7:8). Amos saw this plumb line of the Lord as a strict judgment to separate true faith from false, and he knew that it would be used.

The third element in the prophecy of Amos was his expression of the love of God for the very same people whom He was measuring and judging with the plumb line. There was a difference between other peoples and nations and the people Amos was addressing.

> "Are you not like the Ethiopians to me,
> O people of Israel?" says the Lord,
> "Did I not bring up Israel from the land of Egypt,
> and the Philistines from Caphtor and the Syrians from Kir?
> Behold, the eyes of the Lord God are upon the sinful kingdom,
> and I will destroy it from the surface of the ground;
> except that I will not utterly destroy the house of Jacob," says the Lord.
>
> AMOS 9:7–8

That the covenant people of the Lord were in a special category did not exempt them from being punished for failure to keep the covenant (3:2). But their destruction would not be total. God still had a special plan in mind, a special function within the plan of salvation, for His own covenant people. And though they had been unfaithful, He was faithful: He who had started His work with Abraham would also bring it to completion. This did not imply special national glory. It did not mean that these people stood on a pedestal above other nations, as though they were "better." They would survive to embody God's plan as "two legs or a piece of an ear" survive when the shepherd tries to rescue the sheep from the lion (3:12). Israel could not glory in that; it could only praise God that He rescued them at all.

In the New Testament (Matthew 20), Jesus tells the story of the owner of a vineyard who went into the market place where the laborers gathered and hired some men to work in his vineyard. During the day he went again and hired more, and finally, during the last hour, hired still more. And no matter what time they were hired, all of them received the same wages, the wages of grace. When some of them murmured, the master asked them if he had not the right to do as he pleased with what was his.

In Amos we learn that God is indeed Lord, not a celestial certified public accountant who records the minutiae of our good works and manages this universe according to our wishes and our supposed desserts. What we have is the Lord's gift of grace, not the reward for our "righteousness."

The final outcome of such a view of world history is, unexpectedly, a promise:

> "In that day I will raise up
> the booth of David that is fallen
> and repair its breaches,
> and raise up its ruins,
> and rebuild it as in the days of old; . . .
> Behold the days are coming," says the Lord,
> "when the plowman shall overtake the reaper
> and the treader of grapes him who sows the seed; . . .
> I will plant them upon their land,
> and they shall never again be plucked up
> out of the land which I have given them."
>
> AMOS 9:11, 13, 15

It is essential to the prophecy of Amos to proclaim the restoration of the booth of David. The Christian reader recognizes in Amos the first great prophet who, as the burden-bearer of his time, foresaw the day when the Messianic age would begin. It is a long road, and there can be no bypassing of the strict, basic requirements established by God's law. Amos made the people of his time see themselves on that road, whether they liked it or not. Must not those who claim to speak in the name of this God, who, as we confess, revealed himself fully in Jesus Christ, cry out like Amos, "Let justice roll down like waters, and righteousness like an ever-flowing stream" (5:24)?

IV

HOSEA

THE GRAPES OF LOVE

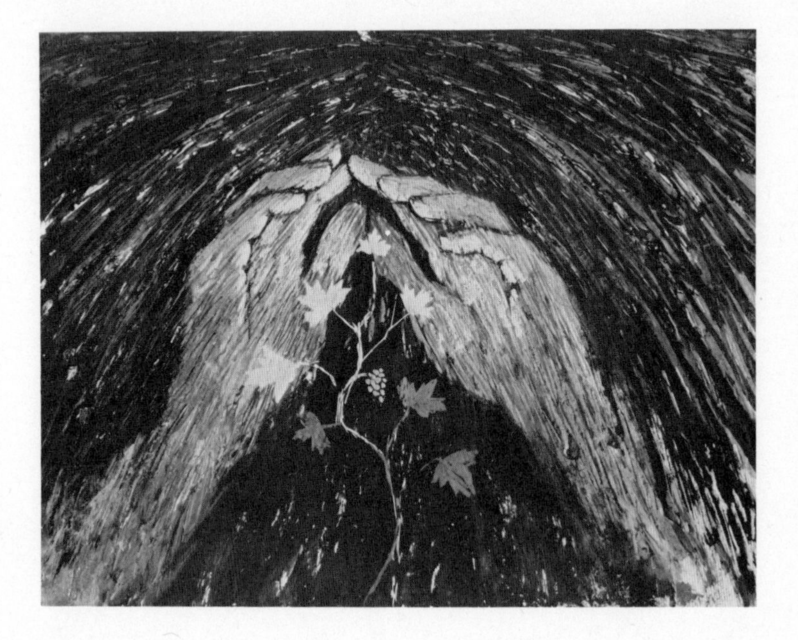

As the branch cannot bear fruit by itself, unless it abides in the vine, neither can you, unless you abide in me.

THE New Testament quotes Hosea thirty times—a witness to the importance of the book of Hosea in the early church. For the first Christian congregations, the books of the Old Testament were their only Bible. It was the Bible Jesus Christ knew and from which He read in the synagogue of Nazareth (Luke 4:16). It is the same collection of books which, in the Easter gospel (Luke 24:27), we see Him expounding to the disciples on their way to Emmaus.

Many present-day Christians limit themselves to using the New Testament, with only occasional reference to the Old to secure "proof-texts" for the truth of the New. Thus, the Old Testament becomes a kind of filing cabinet from which we draw yellowed cards with ancient writing to tell us how right we are. Just as some people seem to think that the Holy Spirit fell asleep shortly after St. Paul and was awakened again by the Reformers, so the Old Testament is sometimes treated as if the Holy Spirit had been slumbering since creation and awoke again only when Jesus Christ was born in the flesh.

One of the services rendered by Hosea was to show that God's work is an unbroken continuum, from the first beginnings of His plan to the final fulfillment He will some day bring to pass. A contemporary of the agitator from the south, Amos, he was at the same time a very different kind of person. His book is sometimes called "the Gospel in the Old Testament." Gospel means "good news"—the good news of God's inexhaustible love, a love that never fails, even in the face of human failure and in spite of human hopelessness.

"Go, take to yourself a wife of harlotry and have children of harlotry, for the land commits great harlotry by forsaking the Lord. So he went and took Gomer, the daughter of Diblaim" (Hosea 1:2–3). So begins the story of Hosea. We are told that these were the first words God addressed to Hosea, and this is one of the most unusual and wrenching calls of all history. There are in the biblical record only a few such commands given to people whom God had singled out for special tasks. There was Abraham, who had to leave kindred and home in a lush and pleasant land to begin life anew in the sterner clime of Palestine. There was Moses, who had to forsake the security of his father-in-law's tent to go to Egypt and lead his people out of slavery. Hosea was chosen to unfold, through his life and his heart-rending marriage, God's unwavering and unsearchable love for His unfaithful people.

In one of the many impressive images that fill the book of Hosea, the Lord says:

> Like grapes in the wilderness,
> I found Israel.
> Like the first fruit on the fig tree,
> in its first season,
> I saw your fathers.
>
> HOSEA 9:10

Hosea is such a grape, plucked and squeezed—not a grape of wrath, but of love. His life and especially his marriage were to be made symbols of God's love for a people who had fallen away.

Hosea was the first of the prophets of Israel to see and describe the relationship of the Lord to Israel in terms of married love. To appreciate what this meant we must see Hosea in the context of his environment. The setting was Canaan, where grape and grain flourished under the hand of Canaanite farmers. When the Israelites emerged from the desert, where they had lived an austere nomad existence with the Lord as their leader and lawgiver, they were keepers of herds and flocks. As they swept in conquest into Canaan, the land of "milk and honey" promised to their fathers, they met a wholly different world, where people lived settled lives in well-built homes, planting and harvesting the fruits of the earth. To these Canaanite farmers, the fertility of the fields, the life-giving rain, the annual increase in calves and kids, and the blessedness of the relationship between man and wife, with the added blessing of many healthy children, were all wrapped up into one package, the key to which was the Canaanite gods and the sacred fertility rites. Apart from the gods and goddesses—the Baalim and the Ashtaroth—agriculture was unthinkable. And the relation between the people and the gods was regarded as intensely sexual. Therefore temple prostitution—sanctified fornication—was a sacred element of Canaanite religion. All nature religions extol the physical act of love in all its aspects. For the Canaanite all troubles and all hopes were embodied in the sexual relationships and marriages of the gods and goddesses. Hosea took this marriage image, with its consequences of sexual union and children resulting from such union, and used it to describe the bond between the Lord and His people.

Hosea's own relationship to Gomer, the "wife of harlotry," became the symbol of the marriage between God and His people in the holy covenant. The very names Hosea gave the children born to Gomer—Jezreel (God Sows), Not Pitied, and Not My People—became a witness to the Lord's love for His people, and to their infidelity. The details of the book of Hosea read like a catalogue of Israel's unbelievable embrace of paganism and idolatry.

> They sin more and more,
>   and make for themselves molten images,
> Idols skilfully made of their silver,
>   all of them the work of craftsmen.
> Sacrifice to these, they say.
>   Men kiss calves!
>
> HOSEA 13:2

Israel had been sent into Canaan with the command to do away with all this, and to establish the sovereignty of the true God over the land He was giving His covenant people. The Israelites proclaimed that sovereignty, to be sure, but many of them saw nothing wrong with having other gods alongside the Lord. They managed to incorporate the Canaanite paganisms into their faith in the Lord and to accept them as a kind of "added attraction." Had not the Baalim and the Ashtaroth given the Canaanite farmer good grain and good wine? Had they not increased his herds and secured the proud fertility of his family? So why not play it safe and let Yahweh be the Lord of all these lesser but extremely useful gods? Such gods could serve well the everyday needs of an agricultural society.

"Harlotry" was the fitting image to express this infidelity. It is easy to see why the Lord should lament:

> My people inquire of a thing of wood,
> and their staff gives them oracles.
> For a spirit of harlotry has led them astray,
> and they have left their God to play the harlot.
> They sacrifice on the tops of the mountains,
> and make offerings upon the hills,
> under oak, poplar, and terebinth,
> because their shade is good.
>
> HOSEA 4:12–13

But "harlotry" was more than a metaphor. It was a vivid and accurate description of what was going on in the daily life of the Israelites—all in the service of religion. The prevalence of sacred prostitution in the midst of Israel has led some scholars to believe that Gomer, Hosea's "wife of harlotry," was a temple prostitute whom Hosea purchased at the command of the Lord (3:1–3). Others believe that Gomer was merely a woman inclined to infidelity and that she forsook Hosea after the birth of their son Jezreel. Others think, on the basis of modern as well as Hebrew morality, that Hosea's marriage is but an allegory, that the Lord would not command His prophet to do anything so immoral as to marry a woman who was a prostitute in fact or by inclination.

This question will never be decided conclusively. We must remember, however, how important symbolic actions were in expressing forcefully the prophets' words. At the command of the Lord, Jeremiah buried a linen waistcloth in the earth so that when he exhumed it, the decay might be a witness that Judah, too, would one day be "good for nothing" (Jeremiah 13:1–11). Isaiah, at the bidding of the Lord, once walked naked through the streets of Jerusalem so that Judah might know that the Egyptians on whom they relied would be led away, "with buttocks uncovered," by the Assyrians (Isaiah 20). Through his tragic marriage, Hosea was called to express Israel's love for, not one God, but all kinds of gods. But what the Lord wanted from Israel was something quite different from the promiscuous or half-hearted love they allotted Him. "I desire steadfast love and not sacrifice, the knowledge of God, rather than burnt offerings" (Hosea 6:6). The Hebrew word for what the Revised Standard Version translates as "steadfast love" is difficult to render into English. Like many key words in the Bible, it was not one in common use. For example, when referring to the creation of the heavens and the earth, the Hebrew Bible does not use the same word it employs to say that man produces something. One word is often used for God's "speaking" and a completely different word for man's speaking. English vocabulary lacks the words to indicate these differences. In Hosea 6, the word we translate as "steadfast love" is a special term used in the Hebrew Bible to express the unshakable loyalty that should bind together the two parties of the covenant. Israel is what it is only as a covenant people, and the covenant means that in His steadfast love God had committed himself unstintingly to the covenant, for man's sake, asking in return the "steadfast love" which means that man gives himself completely to Him. This was an act of God's overwhelming grace and love—to want to belong to man as He wants man to belong completely to Him.

Couldn't this be the finest image of what faith ought to be? Faith is more than a compendium of the writings of learned theologians. Repeating the Apostles' Creed a thousand times is no guarantee that you are a Christian or will become one, even though you may understand clearly the theological and philosophical implications of your words. Words are important, as the work of the prophets testifies, but they are not enough. It is important to note that, in addition to "steadfast love," this verse of Hosea requires "knowledge of God." Here again the English translation is inadequate. What is meant by the Hebrew word is not that knowledge which results from the storing of information in our human memory bank. What is meant is not something to be recited in a catechetical class, important though that may be. Nor is this "knowledge" the fruitful reward inevitably granted to those who read the complete Bible once each year. The kind of knowledge of which Hosea speaks is close to that kind of "knowing" we encounter frequently in the Old Testament in a statement like, "Adam knew Eve his wife," or, in the New Testament, when we are told that Joseph "knew not" his wife Mary. All of us are aware that these are references to sexual union. This most intimate kind of knowing is a knowing, not merely with one's mind, but with one's whole person. Only in genuine love can one really "know" another.

Today we are fascinated with the idea of objectivity. We think it a great achievement to be able to stand aloof, cool and detached, observing the facts and reporting them as they are. That is indeed an achievement. At the same time, is it not true that only those who love their work or what they work with are likely to be genuinely productive or, indeed, even to see the facts? And what is here true in physics, chemistry, mathematics, or any other field of the sciences, is also true for the spiritual life of man. If you do not love your God, your church, your Lord, your Scripture, then your religion is only a conversation piece, devoid of life. You do not really "know" them.

Because Israel had given its love to other gods, it did not really know the Lord. Because the Lord did not seek to be worshiped as were the Baalim, in holy fertility rites, Israel concluded that the Lord was unconcerned about fertility or powerless to grant it. Therefore Israel, who looked to the Baalim for fertile fields and cattle, would have to learn through deprivation Who really gave the increase:

> And she did not know
> that it was I who gave her
> the grain, the wine, and the oil,
> and who lavished upon her silver
> and gold which they used for Baal.
> Therefore I will take back
> my grain in its time,
> and my wine in its season;
> and I will take away my wool and my flax,
> which were used to cover her nakedness.
>
> HOSEA 2:8–9

As Hosea had learned what it meant to be forsaken by his wife, whom he loved in spite of all, so he understood, with the insight—and pain—derived from such knowledge, what would be the consequences of Israel's lack of knowledge and steadfast love:

> There is no faithfulness or kindness,
> and no knowledge of God in the land;
> there is swearing, lying, killing, stealing, and committing adultery;
> they break all bounds and murder follows murder.
> Therefore the land mourns,
> and all who dwell in it languish;
> and also the beasts of the field,
> and the birds of the air;
> and even the fish of the sea are taken away.
> . . . .
> My people are destroyed for lack of knowledge. . . .
>
> HOSEA 4:1–3, 6

Like Amos, Hosea too had to announce the threat posed by Assyria, the instrument of the Lord's wrath. The third child born to Gomer and Hosea was named *Lo-ammi,* that is, "Not my people, for you are not my people, and I am not your God" (1:9). This sounds like a pronouncement of final judgment, like a total divorce, as if the Lord were abandoning Israel to its fate. In dreadful images Hosea paints that fate. In His wrath the Lord is like a beast of prey:

> I will be to them like a lion,
> like a leopard I will lurk beside the way.
> I will fall upon them like a bear robbed of her cubs,
> I will tear open their breast,
> and there I will devour them like a lion,
> as a wild beast would rend them.
> I will destroy you, O Israel;
> who can help you?
>
> HOSEA 13:7–9

Who could help—there was nothing left, no hope, no deliverance. Utter destruction was in store. God would rend and tear like a wild animal. He would attack like the dry rot that attacks wood or like a moth that eats up a piece of fabric (5:12). The Lord would forget His people, who should be cast off and their marriage annulled.

There the story might end, were it not for the Lord's steadfast love. Hosea brings his listeners, and the reader today, to an understanding of the purposes served by the Lord's wrathful and terrible judgment. Strange as it may sound, the prophecy of the wild beast, or of killing dry rot, or of the destructive annulment is intended only to awaken and rejuvenate the people. They were blithely treading the path to destruction, and it was Hosea's job to try to open their eyes. He had a gift for imagery that enabled him to convey the gravity of his hearers' situation by pointing out how ridiculous their behavior was. A striking example is the image he conjures up of a man (Israel) who has aged prematurely, has lost the vigor of his youth, but cavorts as if he were still young: "Gray hairs are sprinkled upon him, and he knows it not" (7:9).

Equally powerful, in its tenderness and beauty, is the imagery Hosea uses to express the Lord's love for His people beyond the disaster toward which they were headed. The Lord will be a healer and a lover; he will be like the dew on a luxuriant plant. And Israel will be like the vine or the fragrant wine it produces:

> I will heal their faithlessness;
> I will love them freely,
> for my anger has turned from them.
> I will be as the dew to Israel;
> he shall blossom as the lily,
> he shall strike root as the poplar;
> his shoots shall spread out;
> his beauty shall be like the olive,
> and his fragrance like Lebanon.
> They shall return and dwell beneath my shadow,
> they shall flourish as a garden;
> they shall blossom as the vine,
> their fragrance shall be like the wine of Lebanon.
>
> HOSEA 14:4–7

Why the shift from an almost unrelieved prophecy of judgment to one of forgiveness and love? The answer appears at the beginning of the book, to keep us from misreading the emphasis on judgment and wrath in the chapters that follow.

Hosea tells us in chapter 2 that God will deal with Israel like the man who has to strip away from the harlot all that makes her what she is. When the Lord has done that, then, says the Lord,

> I will allure her,
> and bring her into the wilderness,
> and speak tenderly to her.
> And there I will give her her vineyards,
> and make the Valley of Achor a door of hope.
> And there she shall answer as in the days of her youth,
> as at the time when she came out of the land of Egypt.
>
> HOSEA 2:14, 15

The shift from destructive wrath to redemptive love was not really a change at all. God's wrath was directed toward Israel's ultimate deliverance. All that God wanted was to strip away what had been covering up the true Israel.

To describe such a deliverance, we might use the term "reformation" as it was originally understood by the Reformers of the sixteenth century and as it has been interpreted in our day by the late Pope John XXIII. Reformation should mean stripping away the layers of trappings that the centuries have allowed to accumulate on the true body of Christ. Reformation is the recovery of the original simplicity of the love between God and man.

We need such reformation. The book of Hosea has much to say, therefore, to our generation, with its astonishing achievements—a shrinking world, unbelievably effective systems of communication, probing of the endless expanse of space, man's whole brilliant conquest of nature. Such achievements frequently crowd out men's thoughts of God, and space-age concerns become a very comfortable substitute for God. God is squeezed out, the victim of a room shortage, because we have it so good.

We should learn from Hosea that we can't fool God. He will make himself heard and felt in spite of all we do to exclude Him or His prophets. We may be unpleasantly surprised by the way He will make himself known. We may be even more surprised to discover there the voice of love, addressing us, stripped now of pretensions and illusions. That voice echoes through the prophecy of Hosea. It rings even clearer in the story of Jesus Christ and His sacrifice for a world that knew Him not.

V

ISAIAH

UNTO US A CHILD IS BORN

To us a child is born, to us a son is given; and the government will be upon his shoulder, and his name will be called Wonderful Counselor, Mighty God, Everlasting Father, Prince of Peace.

IN the early days of the church, persecution descended on the little band of people known as Christians. They believed that Jesus of Nazareth was the *Christos,* that is, the Messiah, the "annointed one," the branch sprung from the tree of David. They were persecuted because the established powers did not like what the Christians were proclaiming about Jesus and could not accept their image of the Messiah. As has often been the case in history, persecution did not overcome, but served to spread the church into Samaria and Galilee, and thence to the remote corners of the world. The story is recorded in the book of Acts.

Among these early Christian missionaries and apostles, we are told in the eighth chapter of Acts, was a man named Philip. On a road leading from Jerusalem to the Mediterranean coast, Philip met a man high up in the court of the queen of Ethiopia. He had been attracted to the Jewish faith, but being a eunuch he was prohibited by Hebrew ordinances (Deuteronomy 23:1) from ever becoming a full-fledged member of the Jewish congregation. When Philip met him, the eunuch was reading a difficult passage in the scroll of Isaiah. Philip interpreted the Isaiah passage in the light of the Christian gospel, and the eunuch asked for baptism and was received into the faith. We are told that he then "went on his way rejoicing."

It represented quite an investment for this man to purchase a scroll. In our Bibles today, the book of Isaiah is very long, with sixty-six chapters, which are confusing when read from start to finish. The reason for this is that although it bears the name of Isaiah, this book is not the work of one man. We must try to picture the Hebrew Scriptures as a library of scrolls of about equal size. In Jewish synagogues today the Scriptures are still read from scrolls like that which the eunuch puzzled over. One scroll contains the Torah ("teaching" or "law"), the first five books of the Bible. The next scroll contains the "earlier prophets"—the books of Joshua through II Kings (our Bibles call these the "historical books"). Then come the "later prophets": the great scroll of Isaiah, followed by the even larger scrolls of Jeremiah and Ezekiel. Daniel is placed toward the end of what is called "the writings," with other portions of Scripture, and the scroll of the twelve smaller prophets completes the picture.

"Isaiah" is represented by one scroll. However, under this name, many men, writing with the same strength of authority, have recorded prophecies; Isaiah's editing disciples have also left their mark. Chapters 1 to 39 seem to belong to one person, or at least to one period. Beginning with chapter 40, a different person, who lived centuries later, speaks to us; further on, in chapters 55 to 66, there are probably still other persons involved. But all of them are Isaiahlike, and in spite of their variant witness there is an inner unity to the book.

The first Isaiah, of chapters 1 to 39, was a man of the city. There was nothing of the rural toughness we find in many of the previous prophets, and again in later ones. For Isaiah, the object of his message was the city of Jerusalem, where the temple of the Lord was located. In chapter 6 is recorded the vision that made Isaiah a prophet. Into this one chapter is compressed practically all that Isaiah wanted to say as a prophet of the Lord. This is not immediately apparent, but by reading the chapters before and after, and by looking into the corresponding verses in the history of Judah and Israel, and by looking at the story of the times, we can see that it is all there.

The chapter begins by mentioning an important event in the life of Judah: "*In the year that King Uzziah died* I saw the Lord sitting upon a throne" (6:1). Isaiah thus dates his vision for his fellow countrymen. For the people of Judah, King Uzziah represented stability, order, and continuity. He had ruled for a long time—more than forty years. To the north, in Israel, one king followed another in rapid succession, and murder, assassination, and quarrels over whose blood was properly royal and whose was not kept the people in a state of unrest. The internal tension, heightened by the growing threat of the dread Assyrians, resulted in wild political upheavals. But to the south, Judah, under Uzziah, prospered. Toward the end of his life, Uzziah became too accustomed to power and tried to invade the sanctuary of the temple as if he were king and priest in one person. He wanted to control all the sources of power. Soon afterward he became leprous, an affliction the chronicler interpreted as a punishment from the Lord (II Chronicles 26:16–21). Still Uzziah's people clung to him, and somehow forgave him his proud reach for the priesthood. Even during the time he was forced to live in isolation, as required by the Hebrew regulations for lepers, the people regarded this king as the guarantor of a stable reign. And with good reason. In II Chronicles, which gives a more detailed picture of Uzziah than does the book of Kings, we read that he had successfully contained the Philistines (II Chronicles 25:6). He had fortified his territories (26:6, 9–10, 15). He had extended his influence into neighboring territories (26:7–8). He built up a formidable professional army (26:11–13) and supplied it with good, even ingenious weapons (26:13–14). The army commanded some of the prosperous trade routes and also protected flocks and herds from foreign marauders. This, plus his fostering of agriculture—"he loved the soil" (26:10)—supplied his people with good food, and enough of it. When compared with the reign of many of the kings of Israel and Judah, that of Uzziah excels.

When Uzziah died, about 742 B.C., it was not clear who would succeed him. It appeared that the people had perhaps venerated King Uzziah more than a human being should be respected and esteemed. Uzziah had become more than God's deputy. When, in a weak moment, he reached for the priesthood, he was doing something that many of his people might have secretly wished him to do. When he died, his death left a great void in Judah.

It was in that year, just a few years after Amos was called to prophesy in the north, that Isaiah saw the Lord seated on a high throne in the temple. Isaiah was obviously a man of considerable importance, able to ask favors of men of standing in Jerusalem (Isaiah 8:2); he was known to the officers of the temple and permitted to go in and out freely. One day while he was in the temple, perhaps during a service, he had a vision. "I saw the Lord sitting upon a throne, high and lifted up;

and his train filled the temple" (6:1). The picture is self-contradictory. The Holy of Holies was the throne room of the Lord, where he reigned invisible. The temple of Solomon was so designed because the God who had made heaven and earth, and was king of the universe, was certainly not contained within the walls of a building. As Isaiah beheld him there in the sanctuary, the train of the Lord's royal garment filled the temple—the Lord was crowded out by the train of his garment, which meant that he was in the temple and yet not in the temple, at one and the same time. If the train of the Lord's garment alone filled the space, where was the Lord? In these opening lines of his great vision Isaiah is telling us that God was truly present as the king in the temple of Jerusalem, and at the same time he was not spacially confined to the temple or to Jerusalem.

Then we are introduced to a liturgy, such as might have been sung daily in the temple by the Levitical singers, who might in fact have been singing during Isaiah's vision. But in the vision the choir is composed of heavenly personnel, the seraphim. These heavenly beings, each with six wings, sing back and forth to one another, in antiphonal responses: "And one called to another and said: 'Holy, holy, holy is the Lord of hosts; the whole earth is full of his glory' " (6:3).

As the scene unfolds before him, the prophet cries out, "Woe is me!"—he is stirred to the depths by the experience of the awesome, insurmountable distance between eternal God, the Creator, and man, the sinner in the flesh of this creation. "I am lost, for I am a man of unclean lips, and I dwell in the midst of a people of unclean lips; for my eyes have seen the King, the Lord of hosts!" (6:5).

Do you remember the New Testament story of the great catch of fish? When the fish fill the nets so they break and the boat begins to sink, Peter falls down at Jesus' knees and cries, "Depart from me, for I am a sinful man, O Lord" (Luke 5:8).

The experience of Gideon is similar. When the angel of the Lord appears to him, Gideon exclaims, "Alas, O Lord God! For now I have seen the angel of the Lord face to face" (Judges 6:22). All these men were suddenly confronted with an overwhelming reminder of their humanity and finitude. Their experience is witness to the way we humans are drawn to our God, our Maker, our Judge, and Savior, and at the same time realize how unworthy we are to come into His presence. This feeling is not unlike a common human experience on a lower level, that of the young man who wants to see the girl he loves but is shy and frightened in her presence. Is this not one measure of genuine love—that we experience our unworthiness before the other and feel that we do not really deserve him or her? Isaiah learned the secret of the words about loving *and* fearing God.

The liturgical mood of chapter 6 continues. With the tongs provided at the altar, one of the seraphim takes a coal and touches Isaiah's mouth with it. Isaiah then hears a voice saying, "Whom shall I send, and who shall go for us?" Isaiah, recognizing that not only is he unworthy, but so are the people to whom he belongs, answers, "Here am I, send me" (6:8).

The prophet, now cleansed, can carry God's message to His covenant people. He is sent to a people that has "tuned out" for so long that no new messages, however forceful or frightful, can get through. The prophet's words, therefore, would only "shut their eyes" and make "their ears heavy"—"lest they see with their eyes, and hear with their ears, and understand with their hearts, and turn and be healed" (6:10). The prophetic word would be to them a word of judgment.

The frightened prophet asks, "How long, O Lord?" (6:11), and is told that destruction will come over the land, desolating cities and houses and scorching the earth many times.

> And though a tenth remain in it,
> it will be burned again,
> like a terebinth or an oak,
> whose stump remains standing
> when it is felled.
>
> ISAIAH 6:13

The prophet is told that the Lord's judgment of His covenant people—and, shall we say, of His church?—will affect not only external things, like cities and houses. There will come a time when even the prophetic word that dulls their hearing will be denied them (8:16–17). To fill the void in their soul, "they will look to the earth, but behold, distress and darkness, the gloom of anguish; and they will be thrust into thick darkness" (8:22).

We shall not delve into the historical and political details of the period in which Isaiah worked because, in all of it, Isaiah stays remarkably the same. He continues to emphasize the majesty of the kingship of God, and warns against reliance on political cleverness. The important thing for Jerusalem is to know that God is king, that His throne is in the temple, and that, therefore, the covenant people's hope can lie only in trust in their king—without condition, without doubting. In Isaiah the meaning and cruciality of faith becomes evident. "If you will not believe, surely you shall not be established" (7:9).

Isaiah expressed this unwavering faith in God the King in two ways. He taught his people that the Lord would send them the leaders they needed. And he taught them the quiet strength of those who know that their fate can be entrusted to God's hands.

Like Hosea and many of the other prophets, Isaiah gave his children symbolic names, as signs of the hand of God. One of these sons, Shearjashub, figures in a word of the Lord to His prophet a few years after the vision in the temple, when Uzziah's grandson Ahaz was king: "Go forth to meet Ahaz, you and Shearjashub, your son, at the end of the conduit of the upper pool on the highway to the Fuller's Field, and say to him, 'Take heed, be quiet, do not fear' " (7:3–4). *Shearjashub* means "a remnant shall return" or "a remnant shall repent." Beyond the destruction and desolation that was coming, Isaiah saw a purged people, a chastened remnant that, in spite of all, would put its trust in the Lord, as Ahaz would not (7:12). Isaiah's son embodied this conviction of the prophet.

Isaiah saw another sign of hope and deliverance: the birth of a child. A child always symbolizes promise and possibility, and this hope burns brightest at its birth. To his generation, Isaiah declared: "Behold, a young woman shall conceive and bear a son, and shall call his name Immanuel" (7:14). Immanu-El, as we recall from the Gospel of Matthew (1:23), means "God with us." The church has traditionally understood this prophecy from Isaiah as pointing to Jesus Christ, the son of the young woman of whom Isaiah spoke. The church has also seen Jesus Christ in these familiar words in a later chapter:

> For to us a child is born,
> to us a son is given;
> and the government will be upon his shoulder,
> and his name will be called
> "Wonderful Counselor, Mighty God,
> Everlasting Father, Prince of Peace."
>
> ISAIAH 9:6

Did Isaiah really see the manger in Bethlehem, the blessed mother Mary and the Christ child, and all that followed? Was his prophecy the announcement of the event which constitutes the beginning of Christianity?

In all honesty we must say that in these texts the prophet seems to be speaking only about the immediate future for his people. He is telling them that the long-awaited successor to David, from the line of David, would soon be born, and before the child was fully grown peace would reign again. With the passing of time one period of history often becomes telescoped into the next. In his own situation, with his historical limitations, Isaiah expressed the hope of the ancient prophecies, that the branch from David's tree would spring forth, to become the ruler who would restore life and healing to the remnant.

Some people are disturbed by Isaiah's word *'almāh,* translated (correctly) in the Revised Standard Version as "young woman," because the New Testament in quoting this passage draws on the Greek translation of the Old Testament and so reads "virgin" (Matthew 1:23). In the Isaiah passage, the reference is to a young woman of marriageable age; the Hebrew word (*'almāh*) places no emphasis on the virginity of the mother and can easily mean a young woman with child (that is, her first child). Would it not be well for Christians to see that the central consideration is the fatherhood of God? Is this not the pivotal truth that Christians intend to express when they call the blessed mother an untouched woman? God alone was to give her the child who would be truly God and truly man. It is not the virginity of Mary, but the fatherhood of God, which is declared in the Incarnation, and we should keep it that way. Otherwise we can easily revert to the same kind of human errors that Isaiah, and other prophets, fought against, namely, that it is man's purity or man's goodness that determines God's actions. It is not. It is God's creative love alone that works restoration.

"Let me sing for my beloved a love song concerning his vineyard," begins one of the many beautiful pieces of poetry in the book of Isaiah. The love song, in chapter 5, sings of the beauty of this vineyard and all the work required to make the vines productive. But then, to the Lord's dismay, the vines yield only wild grapes. The Lord calls on His people—the "vineyard"—to tell Him what He should do or what He should have done. "What more was there to do for my vineyard, that I have not done in it?" (5:4). The love song turns into a cry of distress when the lover sees the object of his love destroying itself: the Lord had "looked for justice, but behold, bloodshed; for righteousness, but behold, a cry!" (5:7). Only judgment can follow:

> And now I will tell you
> what I will do to my vineyard.
> I will remove its hedge,
> and it shall be devoured;
> I will break down its wall,
> and it shall be trampled down.
> I will make it a waster;
> it shall not be pruned or hoed,
> and briers and thorns shall grow up;
> I will also command the clouds
> that they rain no rain upon it.
>
> ISAIAH 5:5–6

In distress the prophet must announce:

> Woe to those who draw iniquity with cords of
> falsehood,
> who draw sin as with cart ropes. . . .
> Woe to those who call evil good
> and good evil,
> who put darkness for light
> and light for darkness,
> who put bitter for sweet
> and sweet for bitter!
> Woe to those who are wise in their own eyes,
> and shrewd in their own sight!
>
> ISAIAH 5:18, 20–21

God, the disappointed lover of His people, would punish; but one day He would send from the house of David One who would save and restore and rebuild. The prophet proclaims that the final outcome is in spite of us, and if we look to the sign of hope and deliverance—the child—we shall see Immanu-El, God with us.

VI

JEREMIAH

ON THE POTTER'S WHEEL

O house of Israel, can I not do with you as this potter has done?

IT is too bad when a man's name becomes synonymous with sadness, sorrow, and lamentations. We have derived an English word, "jeremiad," which is a song of lamentation, grief, and denouncement, from the name Jeremiah. The prophets managed to call their own people all kinds of names, and they used almost every conceivable parable and image to portray their people's breach of faith with the Lord. But it seems that Jeremiah had the gift to do this so intensely and with such repetitive monotony that his own name became a byword—jeremaid.

This play on his name has obscured the fact that Jeremiah was much more than the composer of long lamentations. His career spanned the reigns of five kings, a period of over forty years. He began his career as a prophet as a very young man, as is shown in the opening chapter of the book: "Lord God! Behold, I do not know how to speak, for I am only a youth" (Jeremiah 1:6). The last we hear of him he is in Egypt prophesying against his countrymen who have forced him to flee Judah with them shortly after the fall of Jerusalem. There he must have died—far from home and rejected by his people, in death as in life. That for more than forty years of harassment, persecution, and imprisonment, Jeremiah continued to see the truth and to speak it should have made his name synonymous with perseverance, tenacity, and even stubbornness, rather than with gloom and denunciation.

Before we turn to the story of this man and his message, may I share this very formative experience in my own life. As a young man, I lived with my family in Hamburg, in a quarter of the city which was later completely leveled by the air raids during World War II. Our church was one of the buildings reduced to rubble. The pastor of this church had a special love for the prophet Jeremiah. His fondness for the prophet led him to do something unusual and, at first sight, incomprehensible. It was the year 1932. That summer there were the first signs—telling those who had eyes to see—of what the future held in store. One day that summer our pastor bought a small parcel of land beyond the outskirts of the city. There he erected a small wooden shelter, not a house, but still something solid enough to provide refuge even in bad weather. And he called this place Anathoth. For a long time I did not know why he had chosen that name. Then I began to read Jeremiah, and discovered that he was the son of Hilkiah "of the priests who were in Anathoth in the land of Benjamin" (1:1). I learned that in a time of great trouble, when the future of Judah and of Jerusalem looked its blackest, this man Jeremiah was told by God to buy a field at Anathoth. This was to be a formal purchase, with a goodly amount of silver paid for the ground, a deed written and witnessed, and an official seal attached. The Lord then told the prophet, "Take these deeds, both this sealed deed of purchase and this open deed, and put them in an earthenware vessel, that they may last for a long time. For thus says the Lord of hosts, the God of Israel: 'Houses and fields and vineyards shall again be bought in this land' " (32:14–15). It was an audacious, an absurd thing to do: to go through the formalities of buying land, even paying a good price for it, when a foreign conqueror would soon make such formalities meaningless and send property values plummeting. Jeremiah knew what he was doing though, and so did our pastor.

As the bombings of Hamburg became more severe, the people were told to leave the city, and many were evacuated. Our pastor went to his Anathoth. A week later the church and parsonage and houses and apartments for blocks around were in ruins. When I returned from the front in 1945 our pastor was still living in his Anathoth, coming into the city to begin his work, like a missionary, from scratch. It was then that he explained his purchase of this little piece of real estate, not as a refuge, but as an act of faith like that of Jeremiah who bought his field at Anathoth. He wanted to own a plot of ground in a land that seemed to be totally eclipsed by the forces of evil. He wanted a place that would be a witness to the day when houses and fields and vineyards would again be bought in a land that had returned to normal.

In the purchase of Anathoth, Jeremiah was anything but a

man of jeremiads. This Jeremiah was a man of solid faith in the face of utmost adversity and hopelessness. He not only preached such faith, he demonstrated it by purchasing a piece of land and storing the deed in a safe place. The "earthenware vessel" in which he deposited the deed brings to mind the clay jars in which the Dead Sea scrolls were stored. Such clay vessels would survive in the dry climate of Judah for many centuries. Jeremiah did not know whether he would ever get any use out of that field at Anathoth. It sufficed that the purchase price was for Judean soil which Jeremiah knew would someday revert to Judean hands.

Jeremiah's act was one of those symbolic demonstrations which, as we have seen, characterized the prophets. Pottery figures also in another such instance in the life of Jeremiah. The prophet is commanded by the Lord to go to the potter's house where he is promised a message for his people. "So I went down to the potter's house, and there he was working at his wheel. And the vessel he was making of clay was spoiled in the potter's hand, and he reworked it into another vessel, as it seemed good to the potter to do" (18:3–4). The potter became the symbol for the way God works. We are clay in the hands of God. He fashions us and, if necessary, refashions us, just as the potter sometimes has to rework his clay. With the image of the potter and the clay, Jeremiah gives a realistic insight into the essential difference between God and man. God is creator, He is eternal, He is Lord, and we are but clay in His hands. This is not to say that the message of Jeremiah or biblical teachings in general view man as the helpless victim of a fate he cannot fathom. The Creator's judgments are unsearchable and His ways "past finding out" (Romans 11:33); yet He has not left himself "without witness" (Acts 14:17). Moreover, to His chosen people He sent His messengers, the prophets. The clay in the hands of the potter could not bestir itself and respond to the potter. But the covenant people could. In His love for His creatures, the Lord has given them this ability to respond. This is one aspect of what the Scriptures call the "image of God." We are more than lifeless earth; we are clay into which the breath of God is breathed. This is why God expects so much of us. This is why He looked for a change in the people of Judah: "Behold, like the clay in the potter's hand, so are you in my hand, O house of Israel. If at any time I declare concerning a nation or a kingdom, that I will pluck it up and break down and destroy it, and if that nation, concerning which I have spoken, turns from its evil, I will repent of the evil that I intended to do to it" (Jeremiah 18:6–7).

As we saw in the book of Hosea, the prophet's pronouncements of judgment are not simply expressions of a black, capricious, moody God. If the Lord wills judgment and destruction, it is only in order that He might some day recreate and reshape his people in the manner of the potter at work with the clay. The core of Jeremiah's message is not the lamentation, the "jeremiad," but the promise of a God who wants to restore His people. Could there be any promise more astounding than this: "Behold, the days are coming, says the Lord, when I will make a new covenant with the house of Israel and the house of Judah, not like the covenant which I made with their fathers when I took them by the hand to bring them out of the land of Egypt, my covenant which they broke, though I was their husband, says the Lord. But this is the covenant which I will make with the house of Israel after those days, says the Lord: I will put my law within them, and I will write it upon their hearts; and I will be their God, and they shall be my people. And no longer shall each man teach his neighbor and each his brother, saying, 'Know the Lord,' for they shall all know me, from the least of them to the greatest, says the Lord; for I will forgive their iniquity, and I will remember their sin no more" (31:31–34). A man who could paint such a picture of the future, while everything about him offered little credence to its fulfillment, could be expected to back up his faith in this future by purchasing that plot of ground in Anathoth.

But we expect that of a prophet. Or do we? If we think of the prophet as a superman who immediately and unquestioningly responds to the Lord's word unmindful of the jeers and taunts of his fellow men, Jeremiah shows us how mistaken we are. To his countrymen he was "a fortified city, an iron pillar, and bronze walls" (1:18). But to his "journal," or perhaps to his friend and secretary, Baruch, Jeremiah confided his true feelings. This man, who longed for the friendship of others, laments:

> I have become a laughingstock all the day;
> every one mocks me.
> For whenever I speak, I cry out,
> I shout, "Violence and destruction!"
> For the word of the Lord has become for me
> a reproach and derision all day long.
>
> JEREMIAH 20:7–8

Even those whom he counts as friends betray him:

> For I hear many whispering.
> Terror is on every side!
> "Denounce him! Let us denounce him!"
> say all my familiar friends,
> watching for my fall.
> "Perhaps he will be deceived,
> then we can overcome him,
> and take our revenge on him."
>
> JEREMIAH 20:10

Jeremiah is not simply feeling sorry for himself, however. When he sees what will befall his people, he cries,

> O that my head were waters,
> and my eyes a fountain of tears,
> that I might weep day and night
> for the slain of the daughter
> of my people!
>
> JEREMIAH 9:1

To understand the depth of Jeremiah's sorrow and the pain of his disappointed hopes, we need to look more closely at some of the key events in Judah during Jeremiah's lifetime. In his youth Jeremiah was enthusiastic about the great reformation carried out by Josiah (II Kings 22:23), a youthful king even as Jeremiah was a youthful prophet. But Josiah did not live to carry through further reform. In 609 B.C. he died on the battlefield, slain by the army of Pharaoh Neco. This spelled the end of the reforms, the last attempt from within to restore Judah, its temple, and its worship.

A younger son of Josiah named Jehoahaz became his successor, by popular acclaim, but his open stand against Egypt resulted in his removal by Pharaoh Neco, who then placed Jehoahaz's older brother, Jehoiakim, on the throne. Jehoiakim reigned from 609 to 598 B.C., during which time there was an attempt on Jeremiah's life. When Jeremiah complained to the Lord, he was told that the situation would grow even worse. Some of Jeremiah's most vivid imagery, including the image of the potter and his pottery, was created during Jehoiakim's reign.

Jehoiakim's son, Jehoiachin, was eighteen years old upon ascending the throne and he reigned for only three months until Jerusalem surrendered to Nebuchadnezzar in 598. Jehoiachin and many other Jews were then deported to Babylon, and Judah became a Babylonian vassal state.

Under the vacillating reign of Zedekiah, who was king, by Nebuchadnezzar's sufferance, from 598 to 587, the situation deteriorated steadily. Jeremiah, who announced that it was the Lord who had delivered the power into Nebuchadnezzar's hands (27—29), was persecuted as a traitor (37:11–15). Jerusalem was taken by the Babylonians and razed. Zedekiah and the other leaders were dealt with harshly (39:5–10). Jeremiah, however, was treated kindly by the conquerors (39:11–14; 40:1–6). They seemed to think that, politically speaking, he had been on their side, which of course was a terrible misunderstanding. Jeremiah was not a quisling. He saw in Babylon only God's rod of wrath. It was the Lord's work that concerned him, not who won the war.

All through this kaleidoscope of tragic events Jeremiah continued to sound his warnings. Have you ever labored long and hard over something and then seen it "go up in smoke"? This happened to Jeremiah, literally, in perhaps the first book-burning on record. That Jeremiah was not crushed by it illustrates the perserverance and stubbornness we mentioned at the start. The time was the reign of King Jehoiakim, when no one, least of all the king, seemed to be listening to Jeremiah any more. He had even been barred from the temple because his words were so offensive (36:5). To obtain a hearing the Lord commanded Jeremiah: "Take a scroll and write on it all the words that I have spoken to you against Israel and Judah, and all the nations, from the day I spoke to you, from the day of Josiah until today. It may be that the house of Judah will hear all the evil which I intend to do them, so that everyone may turn from his evil way, and that I may forgive their iniquity and their sin" (36:2–3). His secretary, Baruch, the son of Neriah, did the actual writing, upon Jeremiah's dictation.

When the scroll was finished, Baruch took it to the temple and read it before the crowds that thronged the temple courts on a fast day (36:6). Soon Baruch was being ushered into the presence of the king's counselors, to reread the scroll. Frightened by its contents, they brought the matter to the attention of the king, who requested it be read. Then, in an act of cool and deliberate contempt, the king sliced off the end of the scroll as it was gradually unrolled during the reading and tossed the pieces into the fire, one by one.

The result was simply another scroll! Jeremiah resumed his work and dictated the contents to Baruch a second time. But with this revision "many similar words were added" (36:32), so that the second scroll was longer, and presumably more dire than the first.

This incident explains how portions of the book of Jeremiah were apparently written. It was not only Jeremiah who wrote, but also his secretary Baruch who, in addition to taking dictation from his master, also wrote about him (Jeremiah 26, for example, is a report, probably from Baruch, about the time Jeremiah gave the prophecy recorded in chapter 7). In addition, other hands must have been involved. There is no clear chronological order in the fifty-two chapters. But from this material, augmented and revised by the faithful scribe and later disciples, we get a very good picture of the man Jeremiah.

The last we see of him is as a prophet still without honor, despite the fulfillment of his terrible warnings. It was after the second siege and destruction of Jerusalem mentioned above. Judah was a Babylonian province bereft of its elite. Some of those permitted to remain in Judah came to Jeremiah asking whether they should become exiles in Egypt. "May the Lord be a true and faithful witness against us if we do not act according to all the words with which the Lord your God sends you to us. Whether it is good or evil, we will obey" (42:5–6). But they did not really want the truth. When Jeremiah told them to stay in Judah, they left anyway. Because Jeremiah had not told them what they wanted to hear—this was the sin of Judah during Jeremiah's whole lifetime—they accused him of lying and forced him and Baruch to accompany them into Egypt (43:2–7). There, legend tells us, he was stoned to death by his countrymen.

How many of us could bear the burdens of Jeremiah, continue to speak words of hope, and look to the future in confidence and expectation? We discover in Jeremiah a man who allows himself to be shaped by his Lord as the clay is shaped by the potter; a man who can serve as the Lord's "vessel," even in the face of violent and overwhelming opposition. Jeremiah's life seemed to end in failure. For the true significance of his life and his prophecy to be unfolded, another dimension of meaning was required. That dimension is given in the further history of God's chosen people, in the prophets who follow, and in yet another prophet whose life was also vindicated only on the other side of death.

EZEKIEL

THE VISION OF THE VALLEY

Behold, I will open your graves, and raise you from your graves, O my people; and I will bring you home into the land of Israel.

"GOD makes strong" is the meaning of the name Ezekiel. Many of the proper names in the Hebrew Bible conveyed special meaning to readers in Old Testament times. The message that God makes strong was sorely needed in Ezekiel's day, since this was the period of the Babylonian deportation and the destruction of Jerusalem. Ezekiel, along with the deported ones, was destined to live out his life in a foreign land, without hope of return. How could God make strong, when the original promises of the covenant seemed to be lost? This is the problem central to the book of Ezekiel.

The prophet must have been among the recognized leaders of Judah, specifically of Jerusalem. Nebuchadnezzar, who entered Jerusalem in triumph in 598 B.C., was not interested in destroying the Jewish people. Instead he took with him to Babylonia those who might generate a new uprising in Judah, leaving behind the poor and insignificant (II Kings 24:14) as well as a few of the lesser lights among the nobility. Ezekiel, who was born in Jerusalem during the time of Jeremiah, was taken to Babylonia with Jehoiachin, the king of Judah, as a prisoner and an exile, in the year 598 B.C.

When Samaria had been captured a hundred and some years earlier by the Assyrians, marking the end of the northern kingdom of Israel, the Israelites had not been permitted to keep their identity or to continue their worship and religious traditions. Assimilated into the bloodstream of the land of their deportation, the ten tribes of Israel disappeared from history. In Babylonia, to the contrary, the Judeans were allowed to live together and maintain their separate identity. Some of them were settled by the river Chebar (Ezekiel 1:1, 3; it was really a canal which brought water from the Euphrates River to, and through, the city of Nippur southeast of Babylon). In the small town of Tel-Abib, at the edge of the canal, Ezekiel and his family enjoyed privileges unusual for an exile. He had a house (8:11) and was free to practice his religion, so far as that was possible with the temple so distant or, later, in ruins.

The deportees lived in good-sized settlements. They established their own way of life, sometimes in marked contrast to their pagan environment. They were esteemed as artisans (recall that "craftsmen and smiths" had been chosen for deportation, II Kings 24:14) as well as in many other areas of the Babylonian economy, as the Jewish names in Babylonian archaeological finds indicate. We know that during their stay in Babylonia the Jewish people, their temple destroyed and their sacrifices suspended, created the institution of the synagogue. Here they gathered for worship and instruction from their sacred Scriptures, many of which were now collected and edited. Judaism seems to have been stronger and more conscious of its mission in Babylonia than it had been in the holy city of Jerusalem with its temple and sacrificial system intact.

Ezekiel surely visited Babylon the great, the beautiful. The ruins of this city are impressive and awesome to the visitor even in our day. The remains of the monumental Ishtar gate, of the majestic, mountainlike temple of Marduk (the so-called ziggurat, the biblical tower of Babel), of the still-beautiful processional road have not lost their charm and religious power. It is understandable that the magnificent reliefs of lions, dragons, and other creatures, which decorated the walls and towers of Babylon, would find their way into Ezekiel's visions. Through such visions we see one more example of how God speaks to His people. At a given moment in history and in the language and imagery of the age, God speaks that men may hear and understand the message carried in these earthen vessels.

The book of Ezekiel is clearly structured. The first three chapters relate to Ezekiel's call and commission. Chapters 4 to 24 warn of the impending doom of Judah and Jerusalem; chapters 25 to 32 contain some fiery statements about Judah's neighbors, who will suffer under God's judgment. Thereafter, the tone of the book changes, and chapters 33 to 39 promise the renewal of the Lord's people, while the concluding chapters (40–48) record the vision of the restored temple and the restored community.

In 593 B.C., five years after the deportation (1:2), Ezekiel, a priest and the son of a priest, began his career as a prophet.

Ezekiel, it seems, was thirty years old (1:1) when "the hand of the Lord was laid upon him" (1:3). We are reminded of the Hebrew regulations setting thirty as the minimum age for priests (Numbers 4:3), and of the report in the Gospel of Luke (3:23) that Jesus began his ministry when he was "about thirty years of age." The last prophecy recorded in the book (40:1) is dated 573 B.C. His prophecies covered ten years before the fall of Jerusalem, during which time some deportees were already living in Babylon, and ten years after the destruction of the holy city.

His call came in the midst of a storm. As a great cloud drew near from the north, and the fire of lightning flashed, Ezekiel saw "the likeness of four living creatures. And this was their appearance: they had the form of men, but each had four faces, and each of them had four wings" (1:5–6). These cherubim, which Ezekiel proceeds to describe in detail, are known from both biblical and extrabiblical sources as bearers of the throne of the king or of the god. Here they bear the throne of the Lord, which is described as a chariot with wheels "like the gleaming of a chrysolite; . . . their construction being as it were a wheel within a wheel. . . . The four wheels had rims and they had spokes, and their rims were full of eyes round about" (1:16, 18). Here in the all-seeing presence of the Lord, with the glory of the Lord unveiled to him in a manner reminiscent of Isaiah's vision in the temple, Ezekiel heard the summons of the Lord. "Such was the appearance of the likeness of the glory of the Lord, and when I saw it, I fell upon my face, and I heard the voice of one speaking. And he said to me, son of man, stand upon your feet, and I will speak with you" (1:28; 2:1). The Lord then commissioned Ezekiel as His prophet "to the people of Israel, to a nation of rebels" (2:3). This was a burden Ezekiel would carry for twenty years.

It was a heavy burden. Until the fall of Jerusalem his prophecies of destruction were coldly received. After the fall, his countrymen were more ready to give him a hearing and even to seek his counsel. Today Ezekiel would probably encounter even greater difficulties than in his own day. After the first year of such a career, it is likely that he would be committed to a mental hospital for observation, if not placed in solitary confinement. A man who says of himself, "I sat there overwhelmed among them seven days" (3:15), who admits that he was subject to frequent trances and ecstatic stupors in which he was often unable to speak (3:26; 24:27; 33:21) or even to move (4:4–8), but who when his tongue was loosed then exploded into what seem to us fantastic images and descriptions—such a man we would consider to be ready for psychiatric care. Reading Ezekiel's story may cause us to wonder whether, in our age of tranquilizers and psychotherapy, there would have been any such book. It seems that in our day and age, extravagant or abnormal behavior is not considered to be a permissible sign of possible vision and insight. A person with the depth and intensity of clarity needed to see through human pretenses and self-deceptions is very likely to be labeled "sick" by a society that considers itself "sane" and its "normal" behavior normative and healthy. Some thinkers today urge us to listen for the prophetic note in the words and warnings of those who are psychically ill because the world around them is ill.

The sickness of Judean society infected some of Ezekiel's visions and, at the Lord's command, drove him to abnormal actions. He tells how, in the temple at Jerusalem, he saw "portrayed upon the wall round about . . . all kinds of creeping things, and loathsome beasts, and all the idols of the house of Israel" (8:10)—all things causing Judah's sickness. When Ezekiel's wife, "the delight of his eyes," died, the Lord told him to forgo the usual mourning—he may "sigh, but not aloud"—so that his countrymen will know that one day the Lord will "take from them their stronghold, their joy and glory, the delight of their eyes and their heart's desire." On that day Ezekiel's unusual behavior will be their behavior too: "You shall not mourn or weep, but you shall pine away in your iniquities and groan to one another" (24:15–27).

For all their strangeness and seeming absurdity Ezekiel's words and actions are not unintelligible. His is not a speaking in tongues. Like the other prophets, Ezekiel was also granted the gift of interpretation of his visions. The *word* of the Lord came to him. His trances and visions may have struck Ezekiel dumb, but when his tongue was loosed it was not befuddled. The fact that he was also a priest meant that he was a man of order. He was able to interpret his visions to his contemporaries with precision and unmistakable clarity. Some of his images and expressions have become familiar phrases in the English language: "The city four square" (48:30–35), "the field of dry bones" (37), "wheel within a wheel" (1:16; 10:10).

As did the prophets before him, Ezekiel knew he was called to serve in a particular time and place. The revelation granted him was not beyond and above all time, "for all times," but, rather, for a particular historical situation. This situation, as interpreted by Ezekiel and other prophets, was then frequently found to be significant for the future of the covenant people and the Messianic age to which they looked. As a priest who had probably once been among the clergy at the temple in Jerusalem, Ezekiel was concerned during his whole prophetic career with the state of the temple. We have noted his visit to the temple—whether physically or in a trance is not clear—when he decried the corruption he saw. We have remarked that in his inaugural vision he saw the Lord seated on a mobile throne, a chariot with wheels and wheels within wheels symbolizing that God is not bound to one land, one people, one city, one temple. Later, Ezekiel sees the glory of the Lord depart from the temple and the holy city (9:3; 10:15–19; 11:22–23). Because of the obstinacy of His people, the Lord withdraws His presence. After the destruction of the temple, however, Ezekiel describes the restored temple in great detail (chapters 40–47). He was "a man for all seasons," preaching doom to a stubborn people and consolation to a chastened remnant sitting in exile in Babylonia.

There in Babylonia, Ezekiel must have been supplied with news of the situation in Judah through letters, messengers, or the many rumors that would have been circulating through Babylonian as well as Jewish channels. Communication between the Jews in Palestine and Babylonia was certainly not cut off.

Jeremiah 29 gives the contents of a letter Jeremiah sent from Jerusalem to the deportees living in Babylon. Ezekiel 33:21 tells of the arrival of a Jerusalemite to report to Ezekiel the fall of the city.

Up to the time of the fall, and even after, many of the deportees nourished the nationalistic hope that their exile was only an interim and that the old glory of Judah would soon be restored. After all, was not King Jehoiachin, of the line of David, still alive and in their midst (II Kings 25:27–30)? Even Nebuchadnezzar recognized Jehoiachin as of Davidic lineage. Unearthed clay tablets from the Babylonian court call him the "King of Judah," and jar handles found in Palestine speak of Eliakim, Jehoiachin's successor in Judah, as Jehoiachin's "steward." The opening verses of Ezekiel, too, date his prophecy from "the fifth year of the exile of King Jehoiachin." The exiles must have welcomed each ray of hope for a possible reinstatement of their king and restoration of their kingdom. From the book of Jeremiah (29:7–9, 21–22) we know that two fanatical nationalists who posed as prophets were put to death by the Babylonians. Jeremiah therefore urged the exiles to "take wives," "plant gardens," and "seek the welfare of the city" of Babylon (29:5–7). Ezekiel sounded the same note: resistance or rebellion against Babylon was treason against the Lord, who had ordained Nebuchadnezzar to be the Lord's instrument of judgment on Judah (17:20). According to chapter 17, there is no doubt in Ezekiel's mind that the Judean nationalists were not acting according to the will of God.

The first twenty-two chapters of Ezekiel are not easy to interpret, but a careful reading shows that Ezekiel had to tell his people that the marriage between nationalism and faith was an unholy one. For those living in exile, this must have been difficult to accept.

Nor is it any easier for us to swallow. We are inclined to make our nation's cause the cause of God. For some of us God is a Republican, for others He is a Democrat, and for others simply American. We forget that He is the Lord of the universe, that all people are His children, and that all history is His. Only through tragedy did Judah learn that God's purposes went far beyond the Jewish state. The prophetic voices of men like Jeremiah and Ezekiel prepared the survivors of the destruction of the state to understand the tragedy and to interpret their role as God's people in a new way.

With the fall of Jerusalem, Ezekiel's message changed. The same God who had seemed to turn against His people now said, "As a shepherd seeks out his flock when some of his sheep have been scattered abroad, so will I seek out my sheep" (34:11–12). Parts of this chapter remind one of the Twenty-third Psalm, or of the words of Christ about the good shepherd. When the day of reckoning comes, the Lord "will set up over them one shepherd, my servant David, and he shall feed them: he shall feed them and be their shepherd. And I, the Lord, will be their God, and my servant David shall be prince among them" (34:23–24). The Christian reader sees that much in the Gospels is rooted in this and the following chapters of Ezekiel. It is significant that the Christian interpretation of these chapters accords with their intention, which was not to equate the national with the spiritual. For many at the time of Jesus, the Messianic hope was that the Messianic king would free the nation from Roman bondage and restore it to its former glory. Even many of Jesus' disciples and most faithful followers understood the kingdom of God in political terms at first (Mark 10:35–45; Acts 1:6).

It is against this background of crushed hope, tragedy, and death that we must read Ezekiel's visions of the valley of dry bones, so familiar to us through the Negro spiritual "Dry Bones." The prophet was shown a wide and wild valley barren of life and strewn with dry bones. The Lord asks a question the exiles must often have asked among themselves: "Can these bones live?" Can this scattered and lifeless people revive and live and breathe again? Can life come out of death? "Our bones are dried up, and our hope is lost; we are clean cut off" (37:11). The answer the Lord gives to Ezekiel is: "Prophesy to these bones, and say to them, O dry bones, hear the word of the Lord. Thus says the Lord God to these bones: Behold, I will cause breath to enter you, and you shall live"

(37:4–5). The Lord would give life again, but it was like the life of which Jesus Christ speaks: "Truly, truly, I say to you, unless a grain of wheat falls into the earth and dies, it remains alone; but if it dies, it bears much fruit" (John 12:24). That is the Easter gospel. Those who have been through defeat and death will catch the import of the Lord's words to the exiles: "Behold, I will open your graves, . . . O my people; and I will bring you home into the land of Israel. And you shall know that I am the Lord, when I open your graves, and raise you from your graves, O my people. And I will put my Spirit within you, and you shall live . . ." (37:12–13).

On this climactic note, the book of Ezekiel might end. But Ezekiel the prophet is also a priest. He sees that for a renewed people to live means that they must also worship. It is often said that one can worship God anywhere—in the awesome blackness of the night, in the stillness of the forest, in the vastness of the open plain. This Ezekiel would not accept, for not only might it overlook the discipline and order required for worship, but it would also be fraught with the danger of equating creature and Creator. The Lord is present in the world, but He is *not* the world or any part of it. He is the One who is enthroned above the cherubim (as in Ezekiel's inaugural vision) but who chooses to make His dwelling among men, where and when He pleases. In one of his later visions, Ezekiel sees the temple, which the Lord had once forsaken, restored and refurbished for worship, so that the Lord might dwell there once again (43:1–5). This presence and distance of God, so fundamental to Ezekiel as well as to the rest of the Bible, is expressed in the Lord's Prayer, when Jesus taught His disciples to begin by saying, "Our Father" (which makes God as close as is a father to his children), but then to add, "who art in heaven," to establish that He is truly God. Ezekiel helps us to see that those who worship thus, worship "in spirit and in truth."

VIII

THE SECOND ISAIAH

GOOD NEWS, GOOD NEWS

He was oppressed, and he was afflicted, yet he opened not his mouth; like a lamb that is led to the slaughter.

CHAPTER 4 of the Gospel of Luke tells how, at the beginning of His public career, Jesus went to His home town of Nazareth, where He had lived for something like thirty years. He entered the synagogue one Sabbath, as men were assembled to study the Scriptures. Jesus opened the scroll of the prophet Isaiah and read,

> The Spirit of the Lord God is upon me,
> because the Lord has anointed me
> to bring good tidings to the afflicted;
> he has sent me to bind up the broken-hearted,
> to proclaim liberty to the captives,
> and the opening of the prison to those who are bound;
> to proclaim the year of the Lord's favor,
> and the day of vengeance of our God;
> to comfort all who mourn. . . .
>
> ISAIAH 61:1–2

Then Jesus told the men, "Today this Scripture has been fulfilled in your hearing" (Luke 4:21).

In this encounter with the people of His home town Jesus read from the second half of the scroll of Isaiah, and identified Himself with the anointed one spoken of there, the one who was to bring the good news, the Gospel, to those in need, and to proclaim the beginning of the Messianic age.

This second part of the book of Isaiah, beginning with chapter 40, is often called Second Isaiah. Why do we speak of another, a second, Isaiah or, in the language of the theologians, of Deutero-Isaiah? As we saw in talking about the first Isaiah, our Bible, as inherited from the Hebrew people, has but one scroll bearing the name of Isaiah. The first thirty-nine chapters contain the prophecies of a man who identified himself as Isaiah. When he was prophesying, the temple in Jerusalem was still intact, as were the whole city and the Judean state. Isaiah warns of the rot within Judah and of the enemies that menace her from without. He was commissioned to speak, as we have seen, to a people who would not listen to him. His message was to pronounce the news of doom. The only hope he saw lay in a holy remnant: from the tree that had to be hewn down so only the trunk would remain, a new branch, a new Israel, would grow.

In chapter 40, the Isaiah scroll suddenly takes on a new tone. A different kind of message appears.

> Comfort, comfort my people,
> says your God.
> Speak tenderly to Jerusalem,
> and cry to her
> that her warfare is ended,
> that her iniquity is pardoned.
>
> ISAIAH 40:1–2

This is a prophet who speaks on the far side of disaster. He addresses a people who have lost their state, their city, their temple. His job was to bring to his people the good news that the time of punishment announced by the first Isaiah was over: Jerusalem

> has received from the Lord's hand
> double for all her sins.
>
> ISAIAH 40:2

If we look at the two main divisions of the scroll in this perspective, we recognize that in spite of the one hundred and fifty years separating the first Isaiah from the second, the second one completed what the first one had begun. For both prophets the God proclaimed to Israel is, in the last analysis, the God of good news, the news of love and forgiveness which mean new life shaped by the Lord.

If we search further we find other clear signs that there were two "Isaiahs." (Indeed, the distinctive accents of the second Isaiah are less marked after chapter 55, leading many scholars to see still other hands at work in the final chapters.) Let us look at some of these signs. Beginning with chapter 40, no claim is made that Isaiah wrote any of the prophecies. His name is not mentioned once in all the twenty-seven remaining chapters. Also, in chapters 1 through 39 the foreign power threatening Judah is Assyria. In the second Isaiah, however,

Judah is already in exile, in Babylon now, not Assyria, and an up-and-coming king of Persia, Cyrus, is looked to by the prophet as the one who will overthrow Babylon and thus liberate a captive people. In chapter 45 Cyrus is called the Lord's agent, His "anointed." In chapter 44 the Lord says of him, "He is my shepherd, and he shall fulfill all my purpose."

The language and style of chapters 40 through 55 are also very different from that of the first thirty-nine chapters. This is not only a matter of form, the difference between the diction and verse forms of one poet and another. There is a whole new world of concepts: the voice crying in the wilderness (40:3), the highway through the desert (40:3), the suffering servant (42:1–4; 49:1–6; 50:4–9; 52:13; 53:12), a new Jerusalem (44:26, 28). These were pregnant concepts that influenced the Christian gospel profoundly, adding richness and depth to the apostolic proclamation of Christ.

In chapter 40, the beginning of Second Isaiah, there is a sentence that is especially close to me. When I had finished my studies for the ministry and was ready to preach for the first time, it was in a small church close to the shore of the Baltic Sea. The pulpit had been carved out of a huge oak. I stood in it like some small creature sheltered in a huge container fashioned from wood that had been cut long before the Reformation. If I reached over the edge of the pulpit, my fingers could feel some lettering, four inches high and cut so deeply into the wood that it was still legible. Carved in Latin, the words repeated Isaiah's proclamation: "But the word of our God will stand for ever" (40:8).

This was the time of the German church's struggle with the Nazi government, and it seemed that the end of all good things had come, perhaps even the end of the church. The church had been relegated to a small corner in the theater of Nazism, and those who really preached the gospel, the good news of Jesus Christ, were persecuted, hunted down, and imprisoned. Isaiah's sentence, "But the word of our God will stand for ever," became a sort of password, a reassurance that not even the satanic "millennium" of Adolf Hitler, his "Thousand-Year Reich," could change this prophecy.

The word of our God, continues this passage from Second Isaiah, is the word of the same Lord who created the universe, "who has measured the waters in the hollow of his hand, and marked off the heavens with a span, and clothed the dust of the earth in a measure, and weighed the mountains in scales" (40:12). He who brought His people Israel out of Egypt and led them in the wilderness will once again lead them out of bondage: "In the wilderness prepare the way of the Lord, make straight in the desert a highway for our God" (40:3). In proclaiming God in this way the second Isaiah was heir to the ancient tradition of his people, for all Scripture witnesses to the conviction that it is the same one God who creates, who is the master of history, and within history is the deliverer of His people.

Some people outside the Christian faith, and apparently many Christians, too, misunderstand the doctrine of the Holy Trinity and think that the Christian worships three gods or three versions of one God. Some Christians so highly exalt the person of Jesus Christ that they move rather hurriedly over that part of the Creed which talks about the Creator and creation; nor do they have much to say about the third article of the Creed, concerning the Holy Spirit and his work in the church and in members of the church. The Christian should understand that in the whole of Scripture the creator God and the savior God are one God.

> Have you not known? Have you not heard?
> The Lord is the everlasting God,
> the Creator of the ends of the earth.
> He does not faint or grow weary, . . .
> But they who wait for the Lord shall renew their strength,
> they shall mount up with wings like eagles,
> they shall run and not be weary,
> they shall walk and not faint.
>
> ISAIAH 40:28, 31

This unity of God is at the core of the good news that the second Isaiah announces. It is the creator God who will deliver

His people, leveling the mountains and exalting the valleys to make a royal highway for them through the desert (40:4). When the people cry to Him, says the Lord,

> I will open rivers on the bare heights,
> and fountains in the midst of the valleys;
> I will make the wilderness a pool of water,
> and the dry land springs of water.
>
> ISAIAH 41:18

To bring about the promised deliverance and renewal, the prophet sees a strange figure that has disturbed and puzzled every succeeding generation since. It is "the servant of the Lord," "the suffering servant," the one who would bear "the sin of many," and as the "man of sorrows" would liberate and restore his people. There has been much discussion about this "servant." Is he one person? Or does he represent the remnant of Israel, the minority of the faithful who would fill the gap left by the faithless majority? Is he the Messiah to come, or is even the prophet himself, a sort of servant of God's suffering in behalf of his people?

The "servant songs," as they are called in Second Isaiah, are not as clear from the Christian viewpoint as we might wish them to be. For the reader with the picture of Golgotha in his heart and memory, the fourth Servant Song seems to be a description of Jesus Christ:

> He was despised and rejected by men;
> a man of sorrows, and acquainted with grief;
> and as one from whom men hide their faces
> he was despised, and we esteemed him not.
> Surely he has borne our griefs
> and carried our sorrows;
> yet we esteemed him stricken,
> smitten by God, and afflicted.
> But he was wounded for our transgressions,
> he was bruised for our iniquities;
> upon him was the chastisement that made us whole,
> and with his stripes we are healed.
>
> ISAIAH 53:3–5

In subsequent verses we see the lamb led to slaughter, and the sheep that did not open its mouth before the shearer. This is the servant who would bear in free will, in a genuine sacrifice, the burden for all men.

In Hebrew thought, and in the Hebrew Scriptures, there is no sharp distinction between the individual and the people as a whole. When an individual transgresses, the whole community often suffers. And if one suffers willingly because of sins he has not committed, the community is the beneficiary. This concept of "corporate personality" (as it has been called) helps explain why in the New Testament the community of Jesus Christ is described as a "body," of which Jesus is the head and we are all members. Later, the church fathers talked about the church as the mystical body of the Lord. There is joy in salvation only if it includes our brother, whom the Lord loves as much as He loves us and for whom the servant suffered, as indeed he suffered for us. The suffering of the servant of the Lord binds us together, making of us a community, a new community, with Him as the center.

We often hear that the idea of vicarious suffering, the suffering of the one for the many, is a New Testament concept. That is true, but it is also the subject of the servant poems. Second Isaiah introduced into the Hebrew Bible, and from there into the New Testament world, the recognition of the fact that this is the way the world is constituted. No child is born without endangering the life of the mother. No generation exists without the pains and sorrows of the preceding one, and each generation must render the same service for the next. Nothing great in this world is bought without suffering—of an individual, of a few, or of many.

This is not a morose view of life. The prophet is simply stating that these are the terms on which life is really possible. One must suffer for the others. Some will do so only under protest. But the servant suffers willingly:

> I gave my back to the smiters,
> and my cheeks to those who
> pulled out the beard;

I hid not my face
from shame and spitting.
ISAIAH 50:6

Of such a servant the prophet says, "Yet it was the will of the Lord to bruise him" (53:10). "The Lord has laid on him the iniquity of us all" (53:6).

Golgotha is the direct outcome, the result and consequence of the second Isaiah's prophetic message. The Christian faith is rooted in the Old Testament. And on Golgotha the servant songs sound their fullest and deepest tones.

The message of Second Isaiah, with its opening call to comfort and to speak tenderly to the people who have been punished so long, was really good news. This afflicted people could glimpse the unsearchable riches of the grace of God as the prophet spelled out in detail the guilt offering which the servant was to bring. In the past, sacrificial animals had been offered, according to the priestly ordinances (Leviticus 5); now the servant would offer the full sacrifice by offering himself. Christian tradition calls the day of the sacrifice of Jesus Christ "Good Friday," thus expressing the seeming contradiction in that event. He dies, but His death is sacrificial—the New Testament can therefore call the account of His death "gospel," that is, good news.

The second Isaiah seems to have caught in his prophecies the spirit that should and could establish a basis for mutual understanding between Judaism and Christianity. Even if one does not accept Jesus as the Christ, the idea that only in suffering can new life begin, and that only in the death of the seed can new fruit be generated, should be understood by the people which has suffered so much (too often at Christian hands). And the Christian might well humble himself, not in words but by offering his body as "a living sacrifice" (Romans 12:1), according to the message enunciated by the second Isaiah, and fulfilled in Jesus Christ, that without the death of the One, there is no life.

IX

JOB

THROUGH THE VALLEY OF SHADOWS

How can a man be just before God?

IN the New Testament the book of James (5:11) counts Job among the patient and steadfast men of the Old Testament. "The patience of Job" is proverbial. If we look at the book of Job, however, we discover that Job is anything but patient. At the onset of his sufferings he accepts them at God's hand, it is true: "The Lord gave and the Lord has taken away; blessed be the name of Lord" (1:21). This may be why Job's name has become synonomous with patience. If we read beyond the first two chapters of the book, however, we see a Job who is rebellious and talks back to God. He is not the pious, quiet sufferer, silently bearing his cross.

For some people the important question about the book of Job seems to be whether Job really was a historical figure, whether a person named Job ever existed and underwent all that suffering. But, as with the story of Jonah, the truth of the book of Job lies elsewhere than in a positive answer to that question. It lies in the book's impressive realism, in the way it reflects real life, and is able to take attitudes and ideas that still trouble people today and to put them into the context of the great question: Is God really the God of justice? Is He just, or is He an arbitrary tyrant, and we the victims of His whims?

There are some literary problems connected with the book that should be mentioned first. The bulk of the book (chapters 3–42:6), a series of poetic discourses, is framed in prose (chapters 1–2, 42:7–17). These two sections, poetry and prose, seem to originate in different periods, from different writers. It is also true that there is a kind of unreal ending, because all that Job had lost is returned to him in good measure. After the highly dramatic development of the arguments in the poetic section, it is a letdown to be told that everything works out fine in the end. It does not really matter if one ignores the prose ending, however, because the story up to that point is so powerful that it carries its own weight and provides its own resolution of the problems raised.

Next we must ask why we treat the book of Job among

the prophets. In the usual sense, Job is not a prophet. He is not one in the line of prophets from Elijah to Amos to Jeremiah, nor does his book appear among the prophets in the Hebrew or English Bibles. Yet we may say that the book of Job is prophetical because it reveals a very important aspect of the nature of God, as much as man can ever grasp. Recall that a prophet is someone who proclaims God's will, in three ways. He analyzes the past, puts a spotlight on the present, and indicates what the future will be when seen in the same light. Job asks these three questions in a very personal way: How much does the past mean in respect to my present condition? What does my condition mean now, when it is illumined by God? What shall I do? And all this is under the heading: Is God really a just God?

The opening verses set the scene for the story. "There was a man in the land of Uz, whose name was Job; and that man was blameless and upright, one who feared God, and turned away from evil" (1:1). Other biblical references indicate that Uz lay somewhere in the barren stretches east of Palestine. No one is really sure of its precise location, however, and this vagueness probably fits with the author's purposes: Uz is nowhere, yet everywhere. It sounds far-fetched, too, to hear of a man who "was blameless and upright, one who feared God, and turned away from evil." What is told about him—his seven sons and three daughters, his seven thousand sheep, three thousand camels, and other possessions, how he lived his life (1:2–5)—all sounds too good to be true. But there he was, the good man Job.

Now the scene shifts from earth to heaven, where some remarkable proceedings take place. There is a kind of cabinet meeting in heaven. Among the ministers of God's "cabinet" there appears a special minister entrusted with the portfolio for evil or, more precisely, for accusation or prosecution. He is "The Adversary"—that is what the Hebrew word *satan* means. Satan has a place in God's household! This is the first surprising insight of the book of Job, one of many which are likely to be unsettling to our well-adjusted contemporary Christianity. It is comfortable to think of God as simply good and kind and gentle, always helpful, always forgiving, and somewhat blind to the wrong we do. We like to think of the Evil One as the being on the wrong side of the tracks. And if life is the battleground between these two forces, we sometimes do not know whether God is the superior of the two, because evil is so prevalent. In the book of Job, however, God is at the helm of the ship of state, and Satan is one of His subordinates. Does this mean that God was the originator of Satan? Obviously He had to be, because God created all—heaven and earth, light and darkness, glory and hell. In any complete picture of God—one that tries to take account of the full reality of life—can Satan be an accident that somehow slipped by when God wasn't looking? God can and does use good and evil, night and day, destruction and creation, according to His will and His unsearchable purposes. God is really God in the book of Job.

Satan behaves as we might expect. When the Lord asks him about his whereabouts, he ducks the question and answers pertly that he came "from going to and fro on the earth, and from walking up and down on it" (1:7). This was his way of saying that it was none of God's business. Satan was impudent. He personified contempt of God.

We note that it is the Lord who draws Satan's attention to Job, and not the other way around. It seems that God is doing what, in the Lord's Prayer, we pray that He might not do: "And lead us not into temptation." The difficulty may lie in the word "temptation," the usual English translation here. God does not "tempt" people, but He does test them. As the prophets express it and the psalms sing about it, God does not attempt to seduce us, but to try us, as metal is proved in the fire.

Satan fulfills his role as prosecutor. He suggests that Job's exemplary piety, righteousness, and goodness are nothing but items in trade in his relationship with God. God had always been good to Job; why shouldn't Job love and obey God? "Does Job fear God for nought? Hast thou not put a hedge about him and his house and all that he has, on every side?

Thou hast blessed the work of his hands, and his possessions have increased in the land. But put forth thy hand now and touch all that he has, and he will curse thee to thy face" (1:9–11). Satan claims that Job will completely change his attitude toward God if he experiences a change in his fortunes. God's response is as surprising as are some of the other sentences in this opening chapter: "Behold, all that he has is in your power; only upon himself do not put forth your hand" (1:12).

One after another, messengers of gloom begin to arrive at Job's door. His property has been reduced to nothing, his servants have been slain, his sons and daughters have all died—and suddenly Job is without possessions and without family, except for his wife. Job's reaction to these initial blows dealt by Satan, with God's permission, do not shake his faith. He does not ask, "Why does this have to happen to me?" He is still able to say, "Naked I came from my mother's womb, and naked shall I return; the Lord gave, and the Lord has taken away; blessed be the name of the Lord" (1:21). "In all this," comments the biblical text, "Job did not sin or charge God with wrong" (1:22).

Now another meeting of the heavenly cabinet takes place. After Satan's usual audacious answer to the rather polite inquiry by God, the conversation about Job continues. The Lord points out that despite Satan's assaults Job still remains steadfast (2:3). Satan, who has not been permitted to touch Job himself (1:12), replies: "Skin for skin! All that a man has he will give for his life. But put forth thy hand now, and touch his bone and his flesh, and he will curse thee to thy face" (2:4–5). Once again Satan gets permission to try his worst, but again there is a limitation: he must spare Job's life (2:6). "So Satan went forth from the presence of the Lord, and afflicted Job with loathsome sores from the sole of his foot to the crown of his head" (2:7).

Job's wife found her husband sitting on a heap of ashes, scratching himself with an old potsherd. Job was in the depths of misery, and his wife said: "Do you still hold fast your integrity? Curse God, and die!" (2:9). But Job did not let himself be tempted. He recognized that all he was and all he had was God's gift, and therefore it was God's right and privilege also to take away. "Shall we receive good at the hand of God, and shall we not receive evil?" (2:10b). In the way the biblical text comments on Job's behavior there is a hint of what is to come: "In all this Job did not sin with his lips" (2:10). He still had enough discipline not to put into words what he was feeling, but his heart was filled with resentment, self-pity, self-hatred. And from that point it was not far to hating God.

What we have learned so far is all preparatory. The real drama is only beginning. Three of Job's friends appear. They are named Eliphaz ("God is the Dispenser"), Bildad ("Son of Contention"), and Zophar ("Hairy" or "Rough"). Their names are perhaps intended to signal what they will say to Job. Chapters 3 to 27 contain their addresses to Job and his replies.

Keeping at a hygienic distance from Job, they display the recognized signs of mourning: wailing, tearing their garments, and throwing dust on their heads (2:12). Then they sit down with Job—at a safe distance, no doubt—and no one says a word. Job was the first to break the silence. He cursed the day of his birth; he cursed the night of his conception.

> Why did I not die at birth,
> come forth from the womb and expire?
>
> JOB 3:11

Very politely and carefully Eliphaz replies that he does not want to offend Job. He does not want to step on his neighbor's toes. He would rather not speak, but after such an outburst from Job, how can one hold his peace? (4:2). After this polite beginning Eliphaz recalls how, in the past, so many persons have profited from Job's words of wisdom. But now that distress has come to Job himself, Job seems to have forgotten his wisdom (4:5).

> Think now, who that was innocent ever perished?
> Or where were the upright cut off?
>
> JOB 4:7

He suggests that there must be a reason for Job's predicament: it must be a punishment for past sins. For Eliphaz, God had to stay within the bounds of human logic, human understanding of justice, and the idea of debt and payment, guilt and retribution.

In reply to Eliphaz, Job launches into a long lamentation, culminating in the request for a quick end. He does not really admit that he has done wrong, but if he has, he does not know where and in what way, and he begs his friends to point it out (6:24). He would have preferred to confess a past evil and then to be taken away to the place of no return. But he finds no solace in his friends (6:14–23), no relief in sleep, and his suffering is so intense that he must cry out in bitterness against God.

> If I sin, what do I do to thee, thou watcher of men?
> Why hast thou made me thy mark?
> Why have I become a burden to thee?
> Why dost thou not pardon my transgression
> and take away my iniquity?
> For now I shall lie in the earth;
> thou wilt seek me, but I shall not be.
>
> JOB 7:20–21

Job has made himself an easy mark for Bildad, who can restrain himself no longer:

> How long will you say these things,
> and the words of your mouth be a great wind?
> Does God pervert justice?
> Or does the Almighty pervert the right?
>
> JOB 8:2–3

He points to the wisdom of the fathers (8:8–10) and to nature where there is always a cause for everything (8:11–19). "Behold, God will not reject a blameless man" (8:20). He adds, "He will yet fill your mouth with laughter and your lips with shouting" (8:21). Bildad's argument is that if everything were as Job had said, and if he were really innocent, then he should admit that everything will be fine again.

Job, however, drew the wrong conclusion from Bildad's sermon. This happens often, as we know. In all of Bildad's sermonizing Job heard only, "How can a man be just before God?" (9:2). He was becoming aware of the lack of righteousness and goodness in man, and of the thought that, measured with the yardstick of God, man is a sinner. In spite of what is to come in the many chapters of Job that follow, at this point Job had reached the point that would lead upward and out of his misery, because here he began to understand vaguely that we live only by God's grace.

Zophar did honor to his name. He gives Job no quarter:

> Should your babble silence men,
> and when you mock, shall no one shame you?
> For you say, "My doctrine is pure,
> and I am clean in God's eyes." . . .
> Know then that God exacts of you less than your guilt deserves.
>
> JOB 11:3–4, 6

To sum it up, Job's friends told him with their flowery statements that his sufferings show he must have been quite a sinner before they knew him, or maybe even since, and that he should make a clean breast of his sin. If he humbles himself, God will lift him up (22:21–27). Is not God just?

> He delivers the innocent man;
> you will be delivered through the cleanness of your hands.
>
> JOB 22:30

In their narrow view of God, this was the only solution.

Job has learned that his friends are all "miserable comforters" (16:2). "No doubt you are the people," he says, "and wisdom will die with you" (12:2). He tells them he is not inferior to them and that they have not yet told him anything new (12:3). If they were in his shoes and he in theirs, he could string together the same sort of empty phrases (16:4). His conversation with them, which has ascended to higher and higher levels and probed deeper and deeper, has led to no real conclusion. Is God just? Why must we suffer? Can anyone understand God's ways? Step by step, the stereotyped and self-righteous arguments of his friends are broken down. And slowly Job learns not to listen to his friends, but to address himself to God. He learns not to pity himself, nor to make himself the center of the universe, but to look instead to his Lord. He discovers that God is in the center, and not man, and that the very moment man recognizes himself as being under God, the recovery of faith and the step toward inner health begin. Modern psychology has a wonderful term for this—self-acceptance. In the book of Job, however, it was because Job accepted God as God that he could accept himself as he was. In great labor and pain Job arrived at the prophetic truth that faith means to have the whole universe—including one's life—oriented toward the Lord, from whom everything emanates and to whom finally all returns. The harmony which man so badly needs is guaranteed only by God, and not by man, or by nature, or by anything created.

The closing chapters of Job contain the Lord's dialogue with Job. He begins by saying to Job:

> Gird up your loins like a man,
> I will question you, and you shall declare to me.
> Where were you when I laid the foundation of the earth?
> Tell me, if you have understanding.
>
> JOB 38:3–4

These concluding chapters are a magnificent restatement of the creation accounts in the first book of the Bible. Too often we read the accounts in Genesis as though all that ever will be created has been created, and the huge machinery of the universe rolls on. We like the idea of definitely established laws and fixed forms. We forget that it is more important that God is now, at this moment, a creator. His creation is not static, but dynamic. It is in movement. In human history, in the creative process of nature, in the inexhaustible vastness of the universe, there is God continuously active and present. The final chapters of Job unveil the wonder, the ingenuity, the complexity, and the sheer joy of God's creation.

And so the last chapter of Job can tell us about the man who honestly confessed how much nonsense he had talked and listened to. He admitted that up to the time of his suffering he had heard about God with his ear, but that in the experience of pain and poverty and loneliness he had learned to see the true God (42:5). He repented, as the sinner he was before his God, and accepted God and himself, as God willed. It certainly could not have meant much to Job to regain the riches reported in the prose ending of the book. What were they compared with what he had already received—the real freedom of a person who had been naked before the Almighty and had found peace and had recovered his human dignity at the hand of the Lord?

X

THE BIG FISH STORY

Deliverance belongs to the Lord!

It is difficult enough to swallow the story of Jonah, who was swallowed by the fish, but what is worse, folklore has made of the fish a whale. As every schoolchild knows, a whale cannot swallow an object as big as a man, and if a man were trapped in the belly of a fish for three days and three nights, how would he survive the effect of the digestive juices? And with these remarks, the story of Jonah is dismissed as a fairy tale.

A tale it is, that is true. Anyone who seeks to defend the story of Jonah as a historical account, to be verified and dated in the exacting fashion required by modern historiography and archaeology, will not find much evidence in the book to support him. And to attempt to do so would be to miss completely the truth. The book of Jonah does not purport to be a historical record, nor is it a miracle story of an extraordinary biological event. It does not try to introduce a new species of fish now extinct, a fish large enough to swallow a man. The book of Jonah was written to teach something to a people which had lost its perspective on its calling.

Let us set the stage as one would for a play, for the truth of the book of Jonah is like the truth of a great play, a great novel, or great poetry. The place was Palestine. For the Israelites, returned from Babylon, this narrow strip of land had come to constitute their world. The time: about the fourth century before the birth of Christ. The glory that was once Assyria and Babylon was slowly being obliterated by wind and sand, not to be resurrected until the rise of modern archaeology. The once mighty Persian empire was crumbling before the onslaught of an ambitious young Macedonian named Alexander. Pagan religion and idol worship were pervasive and insistent. And there was this small nation on that narrow strip of land, although its boundaries really extended far beyond the confines of Palestine since the Jews had been scattered all over the world. But whether they lived in Egypt, Persia, or along the Mediterranean, they still thought of Palestine as "home," of Jerusalem as the holy city, and of Abraham as their father.

They knew that Abraham had been called out of the pagan world to live in the south of Palestine in order that he might learn that there is only one God, the maker of heaven and earth.

But the course of history had been tragic for the children of Abraham. Only a small number were left to live together as a distinct people. It is really little wonder that in the ferment of the Mediterranean world the Jews felt they were the only sane and normal people. They had the truth because they had the written word of God, the Torah. There had been some disturbing prophets, but most of what they said could be understood as a reaffirmation of the mission of the Jews. Because no other people had received the revelation on Mount Sinai, and because only the sons of Abraham had the book containing God's revelation, the world became, for them, neatly divided into two groups: those in the right—Israel-Judah—and those in the wrong—everyone else.

Wasn't it quite natural, and human, for the Jewish people to take pride in this heritage? It was a heritage one *could* be proud of. True, there were no great works of art, as produced by other peoples of the Mediterranean (but remember, too, that the Lord had prohibited the making of any images). There was no great empire, and no far-reaching political power and influence (although the kingdom of David and Solomon had once earned the respect of surrounding peoples). There was only the parchment scroll of the words of the one God —but how could anything else be compared with this precious possession, which was far superior to anything produced by other peoples and cultures? One might say that the Hebrews had specialized in the religious treasure of the written word of God, and therefore never really produced much of anything else, and that by the quality of this product, the Scriptures of the Hebrew Bible, they knew themselves to be separated unto the God of the fathers and superior to all other men. In such a situation it was easy to forget that others were also children of the same God, and that Abraham and his children had been set apart only in order that the whole world might be blessed in them.

The book of Jonah is only two pages long, with four chapters, and even the division into chapters is unnecessary because it is one text and one story. As so often in Scripture, it is material that has been retold and polished until only the essential elements remain to narrate the story of the man who could not escape the Lord.

Jonah's name probably means "dove" or "mourning dove," a rather soulful name for a man who had so little compassion. When he was given the opportunity to save a great city from destruction, he declined. But before we judge Jonah we should hear his story.

Is it really so surprising, or unnatural, that when God tells Jonah, "Arise, go to Nineveh, that great city, and cry against it, for their wickedness has come up before me" (Jonah 1:2), Jonah should try to get out of that? Who relishes an unpleasant assignment? So Jonah boarded a ship bound for Tarshish, a port on the Spanish peninsula at the western end of the Mediterranean. It was as though you had been told to go to Cuba and preach to the people of Havana, and instead you took a jet for a junket through Europe. It would be a little further away, but in the opposite direction—and much more enjoyable.

Make no mistake: Jonah was no coward. Fear was not what drove him onto that ship. To set sail on the Great Sea for a port at the other end of the world was hardly a fun cruise. Remember how Paul suffered shipwreck when only a little distance out on that great expanse of water (Acts 27)? The men of the classical world, as they themselves tell us in their writings, did most of their sailing close to shore and thus always near shelter. Sailing to Spain meant crossing a stretch of the open and often angry sea. Jonah was really punishing himself in trying to get away from God's command—not the first or the last time that has happened.

Soon Jonah's ship ran into a bad storm. Everyone on board was excited and fearful—everyone but Jonah, who slept soundly in the hold, contrary to the proverbial statement that a good conscience makes a good pillow. Of course our prophet probably did have an easy conscience: he was very pleased with himself and with his clever move to avoid doing what the Lord had called him to do. He would soon learn, however, what others before and since have discovered—that the Lord is a stern taskmaster who insists that His orders be executed.

The sailors behaved as pagans will. In the grip of fear, they "cried every man unto his god" (1:5). They jettisoned cargo to lighten the ship. Finally, they turned to casting lots to find out who on board had done something so terrible as to call down such wrath from the gods. When the lot fell on Jonah, the sailors confronted him and forced him to take a stand.

Why did Jonah run? Not out of fear, as we have seen. He ran, we are told in the last chapter of the book, because he hated and despised the Ninevites. The Assyrians were famous —or infamous—in the ancient world for their cruelty. If God had decided to wipe them out, why should Jonah try to stay His hand? If Jonah preached to these Assyrians in Nineveh, they might possibly repent and be saved! And why should he, a son of Abraham, share the priceless heritage of his people with those who would surely not treasure it and would probably abuse and corrupt it? Strange? Don't we do this all the time? In our nation there are people whom we refuse to treat as human beings or as Christian brothers at the same time that we cheerfully preach the gospel of Jesus Christ as a gospel for all men and proclaim that in the church "there cannot be Greek and Jew, circumcised and uncircumcised, barbarian, Scythian, slave, free man, but Christ is all, and in all" (Colossians 3:11). Or we wish atom bombs or hydrogen bombs, or fire and brimstone on the Russian and Chinese communists, conveniently forgetting that they also are God's children and that so far hydrogen bombs have not converted anyone to the truth.

In our personal lives, it is so much easier to denounce those who transgress the written or unwritten rules of society, or to imprison those who cannot cope with the rigors of society, than it is to bother about them as humans, as children of the same God and Father of us all. Just that, of course, is one of the living accents of the story of Jesus Christ: because He cared about the lost and the strayed He repeatedly got entangled with publicans, prostitutes, and other public sinners, to the great dismay of the righteous. This lesson of love for those outside the pale is what Jonah has to be taught. Hence the storm that catches up with Jonah in his flight.

In normal circumstances, the veneer of civilization and of common training and habits conceals our true natures rather successfully. In an emergency, however, the basic traits of a man or woman usually emerge. Here we must admire Jonah. When he was confronted by the captain and the crew of the ship, he did not play down his guilt or engage in foolish superstitions with them. Rather, in response to their questions about who he was and where he came from, he identified himself and made a bold confession of faith: "I am a Hebrew; and I fear the Lord, the God of heaven, who made the sea and the dry land" (1:9). From previous remarks, they knew about his flight (1:10), and were more afraid than ever. When they asked him what to do he simply told them, in an amazing display of faith, "Take me up and throw me into the sea; then the sea will quiet down for you; for I know that it is because of me that this great tempest has come upon you" (1:12). After some hesitation they followed his advice and threw Jonah into the raging sea. At once it grew calm, and in a different kind of fear the men in their way recognized the sovereign might of the true God.

Chapter 2 consists of the prayer which Jonah prayed in the belly of the "fish." It is really a piece of poetry, similar to some of the psalms in which pious Hebrews speak of distress as being engulfed in "the flood," "the torrent," "the raging waters" (Psalm 124:3–5). Jonah likens the belly of the fish, deep in the heart of the sea, to the "belly of Sheol" (2:2), the abode of the dead. And there, where the dead were thought to carry on a shadowy existence, cut off from the Lord, the Lord hears Jonah's prayer:

> Out of the belly of Sheol I cried,
> and thou didst hear my voice.
>
> JONAH 2:2

Jonah recounts how the Lord cast him "into the deep, into the heart of the seas," until "weeds were wrapped about my head at the roots of the mountains" (2:3, 5). But when his soul fainted within him, he called on the Lord, for, he says, "Deliverance belongs to the Lord!" (2:9). Jonah's faith was of a kind that trusted in the Lord, in spite of the evidence to the contrary, and confessed Him as one who keeps His covenant and cares for His children even when they are utterly undeserving. The history of Israel and Judah is witness to that kind of faith, and to that kind of covenant-faithfulness on the part of the Lord.

In the Gospels, Jesus Christ refers to Jonah's "three days" in the depths of the sea as "the sign of Jonah," the only "sign" that would be given to his generation. We usually understand this as a reference to the resurrection. There is a difference, to be sure. Jonah ended up in the belly of Sheol because he was running away from God. Jesus Christ died because He was obeying God, and people wanted to be rid of Him. But whether obeying God or disobeying Him, resurrection is worked only by God. And whether you run away from God or abolish Him from your midst, or use any other device to circumvent Him, His will shall yet be done. Jonah surely knew that, but now he had seen it confirmed.

"And the Lord spoke to the fish, and it vomited out Jonah upon the dry land" (2:10). And now disaster, real disaster, entered Jonah's life.

He headed for Nineveh, to do his job. When he got there, he "began to go into the city, going a day's journey. And he cried, 'Yet forty days, and Nineveh shall be overthrown!' " (3:4). Then the terrible thing happened. The unexpected outcome was precisely what Jonah had dreaded all along. The Ninevites really listened! From the king on down they forsook their wickedness and amended their evil ways. But if they accepted the grace offered them by God, then that grace was no longer reserved exclusively for that people which, by long-standing tradition, was the sole recipient of God's love and the only true people of the covenant. And this is why Jonah was vexed, extremely vexed. In a modern play, he is portrayed as a clown who jumps around on the stage in a rage, looking very silly in his desire to see Nineveh utterly destroyed. The biblical text is more sober. It says tersely, "But it displeased Jonah exceedingly, and he was angry" (4:1). He points out to the Lord that he [Jonah] knew what he had been doing when he fled his assignment: "I pray thee, Lord, is not this what I said when I was yet in my country? That is why I made haste to flee to Tarshish; for I knew that thou art a gracious God and merciful, slow to anger, and abounding in steadfast love, and repentest of evil" (4:2). The Lord's compassion for the Ninevites so vexes Jonah that he would rather die than live with a Lord who pities such people (4:3).

Jonah was typically human. He was angry with God, with the world, with the Ninevites, because, he, Jonah, was losing his precious superiority. He had to come down from his high perch and accept the fact that he stood before God on the same ground as the Ninevites. He had to accept the fact that, ultimately, he too lived by grace alone. Nobody likes to admit this. Isn't it a wonderful feeling to belong to a religious group of which one can say, "I am in and everybody else is out"? Isn't it a great feeling to have the right admission ticket to heaven?

This is what makes Jonah and his story so real and so true—even if he is not the same Jonah mentioned in II Kings 14:25 as the son of Amittai, during the kingship of Jeroboam II in the eighth century B.C. The truth of the book lies also in its witness to the free and untrammeled grace of God. As the covenant people, Israel was to be only a channel for the revelation of this love to men. As the language and style of the book indicate rather plainly, the book was written much later than the time of Jonah, the son of Amittai. It was put down in writing at a time when Jewish fear of the idolatry against which the prophets had thundered was so intense that it led the Jews to a strict separation from the Gentiles, who gave themselves to such idol worship. It has been suggested that the name "Jonah" was chosen because *jonah,* "dove," is a symbolic name for Israel (Hosea 11:11). To ask, then, whether the prophet was really the son of Amittai and whether he was really swallowed by a great fish is to look for the truth of the book elsewhere than where the author intended. That would be to miss the whole point of the book and its real message.

What does the author want to tell us? First, that this world does not consist of the elect and the damned, the blacks and the whites, the ins and the outs. It consists, rather, of people who are, in the sight of God, only more or less gray, because all are sinners, all are tainted, and not what they ought to be. And this Lord God who created heaven and earth, but chose a special people, loves all exclusive-minded men. No human being, neither Jonah nor any exclusive-minded Christian, has the right to tell God whom He may exclude and whom He may accept. We may not like the inclusiveness of God's love, but there is not much sense in complaining, as did Jonah, because God does love all His children.

The second lesson is that God especially loves those who need His love most, those who are at the bottom—the sinners. Christ loved the "sick," as He called them, and did not expect much response to His message on the part of the self-assured, self-righteous possessors of God's grace (Mark 2:17).

The right beginning, therefore, is to forget our own importance, and to see ourselves as humble messengers of a truth greater than any of us. This is what God tries to get Jonah to see. After Jonah has poured out his vexation to the Lord, he goes outside the city and erects a temporary shelter to protect himself from the sun's rays. There, in the shade of his booth, he broods. Although for himself he covets relief from the burning sun, he still harbors the hope that the great holocaust will fall upon Nineveh. Jonah wants to be away from the city when it happens, but still near enough to witness it. While he is waiting, a plant grows up next to his booth, providing him with cool, green shade after the foliage of the booth has withered. The world was gradually assuming shape again. But then God sends a worm which attacks the plant, so that it withers away. A sultry east wind stifles Jonah and the sun beats down upon his head. Once again Jonah is angry with God, with the Ninevites, and with the wind. Once again he says, "It is better for me to die than to live" (4:8). And now the Lord makes His point: "You pity the plant, for which you did not labor, nor did you make it grow, which came into being in a night, and perished in a night. And should not I pity Nineveh, that great city, in which there are more than a hundred and twenty thousand persons who do not know their right hand from their left [that is, small children] and also much cattle?" (4:10–11).

Here the book of Jonah ends. Apparently God was more concerned with saving wicked Nineveh (including even the cattle in the city!) than He was with His own self-righteous prophet. But His tender concern for Jonah, even after he has carried out the Lord's assignment, is remarkable. How Jonah reacted, whether he repented, as the people of Nineveh had, we are not told. Perhaps that is because the last verse of the book, the Lord's question to Jonah, is addressed also to the reader.

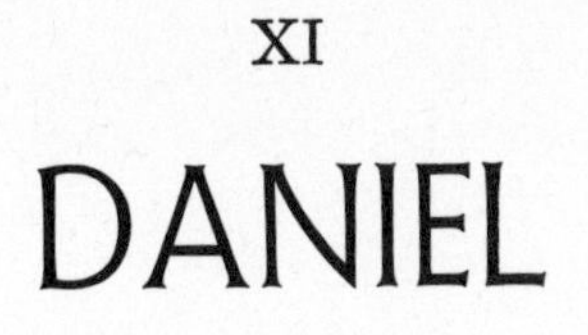

XI

DANIEL

THE WORLD POLITICS OF GOD

Our God whom we serve is able to deliver us from the burning fiery furnace.

"DANIEL" is a kind of household name, if only because of the folk songs in which he figures. The book that bears his name is filled with strange dreams, strange kings, and even stranger beasts. To be honest, it is one of those books many of us would rather avoid. But there are also many people who revel in its obscurities and its hidden meanings. It is a book from which professional soothsayers in every generation have reaped a rich harvest.

The Jewish people do not place Daniel among the prophets. They list the book in what they call "The Writings," that is, books considered valuable and necessary but not of equal importance with the prophets. The men who determined the sequence of the books in our Old Testament apparently did not want Daniel to stand in the same list with Isaiah, Jeremiah, Ezekiel, and the other great prophets.

A prophet, as we have seen, originally was not one who spent his time trying to plan the future. He directed his hearers to the future only insofar as it would or should influence their immediate behavior. If they did not heed his warning, the future would bring destruction and death. Where people turned a deaf ear, the prophet looked to a time when men would hearken to the Lord and offer Him willing obedience. Because God is the Lord of history He would bring His purposes to pass. But the present was the prophet's chief concern.

Let us suppose that one were to isolate and heavily underscore the prophets' faith in a *future fulfillment* of history, based on their insistence that God is the Lord of history. Further, suppose that one were to try to unravel the riddle of the present by a whole series of elaborate and bizarre clues to the future. Then one would have a late Jewish offspring of prophecy commonly called "apocalyptic" literature, from the Greek word *apokaluptein,* meaning to unveil. The book of Daniel in the Old Testament and the book of Revelation in the New Testament belong to this category of literature. For the writers of a book like Daniel, the world was the scene of a great cosmic drama, where events moved according to a definite, divine plan. The writer of apocalyptic literature tried to pull away the veil concealing this plan, to peek behind the scenes and interpret the future to people living in a troubled present. The interpretation is often as obscure as the future itself, however. There are two reasons for this.

One is that the writer of apocalyptic literature is writing to console and give heart to people suffering oppression or persecution. He writes in code, therefore, so his readers will understand but their persecutors will not. Thus the writer of Daniel refers to the petty tyrant oppressing the Jews, Antiochus Epiphanes, as "a little horn" (8:9) that struts on the earth for a brief hour. The writer paints a broad panorama of the rise and fall of mighty empires—Babylon, Persia, Greece—so that in their present distress his readers might know that the Lord "is the living God, enduring for ever; his kingdom shall never be destroyed, and his dominion shall be to the end" (6:26). Here we recognize the accents of the prophets and recall the second Isaiah's affirmation that the Lord "brings princes to nought, and makes the rulers of the earth as nothing" (Isaiah 40:23). To a king like Antiochus Epiphanes the book of Daniel would have appeared to be subversive literature, just as many Christian sermons and books proclaiming the Lord's sovereignty were considered dangerous by the rulers of Hitler's Third Reich.

The second reason for the obscurity of the apocalyptic books is that the writers were struggling to bring to expression something no one had yet experienced or seen. Their books are a stammering about the vast miracle of the yet unseen. In our time, we are often baffled by contemporary art. There are those artists who do not try to show forms on canvas as they would appear in a photographic print. The artist tries, instead, to see behind the forms. He asks what they mean. And because what he sees is often entangled and ambiguous, like life itself, his brush often moves like the tongue of a stammering child overwhelmed by what he sees, wrestling with a new world yet in the process of discovery.

It is against this background that we must read the book of Daniel. It is filled with puzzling names and numbers, cryptic allusions, and bizarre imagery. But in this tangle of visions and revelations we also meet some young Hebrews, among them a straightforward and faithful young man named Daniel. Our Jewish brothers would call him a *Hasid,* a pious one. They were those Jews who, in the time of Antiochus Epiphanes (175–163 B.C.) and later, led the Jewish resistance to attempts to make them worship other gods in addition to the Lord or to transgress the Torah, the law of Moses. The writer of Daniel was in all likelihood one of the "pious ones," who were particularly incensed that Antiochus, who had inherited a piece of Alexander the Great's empire, had made it a crime to observe the Jewish law and had even offered swine's flesh on the altar in the temple ("the abomination of desolation," 9:27; 11:31; 12:11)!

The first six chapters of Daniel show us how Daniel and his three friends keep the law in the face of royal decrees forbidding it. Because they have the Lord as their God, they need not cringe before the rulers of this world. They know that the Lord will shut the mouths of wild beasts and deliver the faithful from the fiery furnace of affliction. It is the act of deliverance, and not the Lord's power to alter the properties of fire, that is the point of the story of the three men in the fiery furnace.

The scene of the story is Babylon, and the tyrant is King Nebuchadnezzar (although the reader would understand that Nebuchadnezzar only stood for present tyrants, like Antiochus). Nebuchadnezzar set up a huge image made of gold, not because he was so religious but because he could use the image to have his subjects bow down before something that he, Nebuchadnezzar, had set up. Anyone who attended one of the big congresses of Nazi Germany and saw the emotions aroused by the swastika, the slogans, and the speeches knows that such demands are not limited to the days of Nebuchadnezzar or Antiochus. At a given signal everyone in Nebuchadnezzar's domain was to bow down. It would have given the king a great sense of power to know that at the same moment the court around him bowed down before the image, everyone in his kingdom would be doing the same.

But what about the three young Hebrews? "At that time," we are told, "certain Chaldeans came forward and maliciously accused the Jews. They said to King Nebuchadnezzar, 'O king, live for ever! You, O king, have made a decree that every man . . . shall fall down and worship the golden image; and whoever does not fall down and worship it shall be cast into a burning fiery furnace. There are certain Jews whom you have appointed over the affairs of the province of Babylon: Shadrach, Meshach, and Abednego. These men, O king, pay no heed to you; they do not serve the golden image which you have set up' " (3:8–12).

The tune of anti-Semitism is poorly disguised. The Chaldeans sound as though they are acting from religious motives, but theirs is really a political move. They wanted to be rid of competition. In the previous chapters of Daniel we have been told that because these young Jews had proved themselves to be wiser and more helpful than anyone else in Nebuchadnezzar's realm they had been elevated to high positions. When the king hears the Chaldeans' report, however, he is enraged, again not for religious reasons. Or shall we say it really was a religious matter? It was a question of who was the highest authority, God and His revelation, or a king and his idol. Forgetting the proved merits of the three Hebrews, and for the sake of his own dignity and his own power, the king insists on a choice. It was either he or their God.

The forthright way in which Shadrach, Meshach, and Abednego answered the king is refreshing. "O Nebuchadnezzar, we have no need to answer you in this matter. If it be so, our God whom we serve is able to deliver us from the burning fiery furnace; and he will deliver us out of your hand, O king. But if not, be it known to you, O king, that we will not serve your gods or worship the golden image which you have set up" (3:16–18). This was the kind of courage that the writer of Daniel wanted his readers to have, and everything else in his book is of secondary importance. There is no hatred for Nebuchadnezzar in the reply of these young men. There is not even hatred for their denouncers. Their courage was the result of their faith in the Lord as "the Most High God":

man swallowed by a whale. Just as we saw that the truth of the book of Jonah lies not in the reporting of an incredible fish story, so the truth of the book of Daniel lies not in the scrupulousness with which it records distant events but, rather, in its interpretation of these events for its generation, and for any generation that knows that mailed fist of the tyrant. The writer of Daniel is assuring his readers that on the vast canvas of empires, kings, and nations, the faithful will be kept by the Lord until the end of days.

The young Hebrew, Daniel, is taken as an example of this kind of faith. Brought to the Babylonian court as one of the deportees from Jerusalem in 598 B.C., he and his three friends refuse to eat the food and the wine allotted them from the king's table, because it is not "kosher." Only the dietary law is at stake, but Daniel refuses to budge, for what was really at issue was whom Daniel would worship. He does not make a big scene, however. As one of the sayings of Jesus counsels, he was as clever as a serpent but yet kept his innocence. He disguised the whole problem in a kind of contest: "Test your servants for ten days. Let us be given vegetables to eat and water to drink. Then let our appearance, and the appearance of the youths who ate the king's rich food, be observed by you, and according to what you see, deal with your servants" (1:12–13). Daniel and his friends emerge from the test healthier and in better condition than anyone else at the king's court.

Thus, the past that Daniel experienced at Nebuchadnezzar's court is presented in the book of Daniel as a parallel to and a foreshadowing of what would happen in a much worse form under Antiochus Epiphanes. In this story of Daniel the faithful would find clarification and interpretation of their own situation. Is not this what the prophets always have done? To evaluate the past today, and to interpret the present in the light of God's will, and thus to offer strength and guidance for the morrow? Daniel's book is certainly different from the writings of the previous prophets, but the spirit is the same.

This same spirit is evident in the second half of Daniel's book, which contains a sequence of "dreams and visions of his [Daniel's] head as he lay in his bed" (7:1). Four such visions are related. Strange images, parts of men and of beasts, elements not used in their normal combinations, are used to signify more than meets the eye. The writer paints his huge canvas with a precise code of forms and shapes, perfectly clear to himself and to the initiated, but hidden to the outsider. It is fine to declare forthrightly what is true and must be said, but there is no sense in needlessly inviting the sword of the executioner.

Daniel's visions, with their dramatic sequence of empires, show that the kingdom of God will triumph in the end. In chapter 7 we see four beasts emerging from the sea, from the chaos and abysmal depth out of which the forces of destruction are always struggling to rise. A heavenly interpreter tells Daniel that the four beasts represent four empires (7:17). The empire of Babylon is portrayed as a lion with the wings of an eagle; other strange beasts represent the empires of the Medes, the Persians, and the successors of Alexander the Great. This last beast has ten horns, among which there sprouts a little horn, "and in this horn there were eyes like the eyes of a man, and a mouth speaking great things" (7:8). We know from a passage in the Sibylline Oracles (written around 140 B.C.) that the "ten horns" refer to the ten kings before Antiochus Epiphanes, who is the little horn with the loud mouth.

Then in an impressive heavenly court, the Ancient of Days pronounces judgment on the four beasts. Each is allotted only a fixed period of dominion. The last beast, too, with the ten horns and the one, would be destroyed. Out of the clouds of heaven

> there came one like a son of man,
> and he came to the Ancient of Days
> and was presented before him.
> And to him was given dominion
> and glory and kingdom,
> that all peoples, nations and languages
> should serve him;
> his dominion is an everlasting dominion,
> which shall not pass away,

and his kingdom one
that shall not be destroyed.

DANIEL 7:13–14

The Christian reader recognizes the close relation of such references to the "Son of man" terminology of the Gospels. In this obvious source of much Christian theology, we see the Son of man not as an individual but as a collective figure, a reminder of the corporate nature of the individual's relation to God.

The other three visions are similar to the first—the powers opposing God are allowed free rein for a season but are then checked or destroyed. In chapter 8 the Christian reader will find it meaningful that the interpreter of the second vision, the angel Gabriel, is the same as the one named in the Gospel of Luke as the bearer of the announcement that the day of the Messiah was about to dawn.

In the third vision (chapter 9), there is a significant reinterpretation of Jeremiah's reference to the seventy years of exile (Jeremiah 25:11–12; 29:10). In response to Daniel's prayer for his people, and for clarification of the "seventy years" (9:2), Gabriel is sent to tell him that the seventy years are really seventy weeks of years, that is, four hundred and ninety years. In the last half of the last of these seventy weeks of years Antiochus would "cause sacrifice and offering to cease" (9:27), that is, would attempt to wipe out the worship of the Lord and replace it with the worship of Zeus. That Antiochus' days would soon end, Daniel learns from the heavenly messenger.

The writer of Daniel lived over two thousand years ago, and yet his book sees his time as standing on the threshhold of the end time. We could say that Daniel erred, or that in times of abnormal pressure, a minority group found consolation and strength in the hope that the end was near.

Or we could offer a third view, which is to recognize in Daniel one of the many writers who see their own time as the final, eschatalogical time because it will be the end of them and their generation.

All of Daniel's visions come to a focus around this same

affirmation. There are amazingly precise references to details of Daniel's contemporary situation, all seen under the aspect of the last days. This is the other side of Daniel's apocalyptic prophecy, that the last day is really always near at hand. According to Daniel, man lives in his environment as does the unborn child—waiting. "And there shall be a time of trouble, such as never has been since there was a nation, till that time" (12:1). It is a painful experience to live in the presence of the Lord of history. "But go your way till the end," Daniel is told, "and you shall rest, and shall stand in your allotted place at the end of the days" (12:13). Thus closes the book of Daniel.

For each generation, and for each time, it is the last day, and we can only go our way, the way of the Lord, till the end. Then we can rest after our labor is done, and we will have our place when God's plan is completed.

XII

THE REVELATION TO JOHN

COMPLETE RENOVATION

Now the salvation . . . of our God and the authority of his Christ have come.

APPARENTLY the name "John" was very common in New Testament times, as was the name "Jesus" (or, in its Hebrew form, "Joshua"). It is a distortion to think of the names of the New Testament as unusual, and to consider their sound extraordinary. Most of the men involved in the story of the New Testament had common, ordinary names. This is not surprising, because the Lord selected His followers from the ranks of ordinary people. It reminds us of the fact that the archaeological finds at Ur unearthed homesites of not one Avram, but of several. When reading the Bible we must realize that we are reading about actual, everyday people who are very much like their contemporaries.

Who are these New Testament personalities named John? First, there is he who appears as the forerunner of Jesus Christ. We might call him the last representative of the Hebrew Bible, for he says of himself that he is "the voice of one crying in the wilderness: Prepare the way of the Lord" (Mark 1:3). This John is understood by New Testament writers to be the prophet preceding the Messiah, His herald. When John was beheaded by Herod, his function had already been accomplished, for the Christ had appeared on the scene.

Then there was John the disciple, son of Zebedee and brother of James. The tradition of the church has identified him with the man the Gospel of John calls the disciple "whom Jesus loved." This disciple, says the Gospel of John, was "known to the high priest" (18:15) and so was able to gain access to the court of the high priest, both for himself and for Peter (John 18:15–16). He was the disciple who sat nearest to Jesus at the Last Supper and was able to ask Him questions no one else could ask (13:23 ff.). He was also the disciple to whom the blessed mother Mary was entrusted (19:26–27). The Fourth Gospel, which the church's tradition ascribes to this John, is the one with the profoundest understanding of a Christ who is, in the complete sense of the word, "the Son of the living God."

The same image of a cosmic, all-encompassing Jesus Christ

is conveyed by the John of the book of Revelation. He has been called John the Divine, that is, the theologian, the one learned about God. To a reader of the original Greek text of Revelation it is clear that the writer of Revelation is not the same John as the writer of the Gospel of John or of the Letters of John. The language is different, the imagery is different, and most important, the book of Revelation only once mentions the birth of the Child (12:5), and refers only a few times to the sacrificial death of the Christ (5:6, 9; 11:8; 13:8), with no other reference to His life. Such omissions would be most unlikely for a man who knew the Lord, loved the story of His life, and wrote a Gospel about Him.

The book of Revelation is not very long, and does not require much time to read. But to fully understand it is quite another matter. Even after centuries of study and interpretation much of the message remains obscure, and we shall have to be selective and take from it only a shining facet here and there. The Old Testament begins with the sentence, "In the beginning, God created the heavens and the earth" (Genesis 1:1). The New Testament ends with a book that attempts to tell us about the new heaven and the new earth, which will come in fulfillment of God's plan. We might say that the book of Revelation is the unfolding of the last Genesis, of the second creation, of the new beginning, so that this last book of the New Testament concludes what is recorded in the first book of the Old. Between Genesis and Revelation is the recorded expanse of salvation history. Once we understand this, we need not be overly disturbed when we encounter obscurities in the book of Revelation. It is a book filled with references to signs and portents in the heavens, strange beasts, mysterious numbers, secret messages in code to the reader—all references difficult to understand or decipher and many of them subject to quite diverse interpretations. It is a book similar to Daniel, written during a time of persecution to strengthen the faith of the afflicted; a book that conceals as well as it reveals. Like all divine revelation, it is always the revelation of a God too great to be captured by language. The reader will quickly discern that John wrestled with something that was too big for him to handle. He tells us that the content of the book was given him "in the Spirit," by one who described himself as "the Alpha and the Omega," "who is and who was and who is to come, the Almighty" (1:8).

In the opening chapter we learn that John was on Patmos, one of the small islands off the coast of Asia Minor opposite Miletus. We know that this island was used by the Romans as a place of exile for political criminals and others. The bleak and rocky isle with its jagged shoreline effectively cut the exiles off from the rest of the world. But such a place was exactly suited for seeing behind the veil that cloaks human existence. "I was in the Spirit on the Lord's Day," writes John (1:10), which meant that he was not bound to his body on the island surrounded by the waves of the Mediterranean, but that, as with Ezekiel and Daniel, the ordinary barriers of time and space were lifted. Thus, John was enabled to "see" (a word he uses frequently) scenes and figures and creatures apart from their usual physical dimensions and characteristics.

At first this special vision of John's is not much in evidence. Chapters 2 and 3, which contain seven letters to seven churches, seem normal enough. These churches all were located in the Roman province of Asia, the area which today we call Asia Minor. The seven letters provide fascinating reading, and are still very instructive for present-day congregations. They range from the praise for the bright star of Philadelphia (3:7–13) to the dark shadow cast over Laodicea (3:14–19). It is important to note that these churches are located in Asia, because it forms the geographical background for the rest of the book.

There had already been severe persecution of Christians under Nero (A.D. 54–68), but his attack against the new faith was not on theological grounds, if we may put it that way. Nero simply needed scapegoats, and the Christians were conveniently at hand. Persecution in the true sense of the word began only with Domitian (A.D. 81–96). He proclaimed himself the divine emperor and insisted on being called "master and god." In the year 95, in the city of Rome, members of the imperial household were found guilty of the crime of godlessness. This did not mean they did not believe in a god. It meant that they did not recognize the new divinity, the emperor. The emperor cult was especially enforced in Asia, and probably was well accepted by the pagan people. A new temple for Domitian was built in Ephesus. In simple terms, it was a question of who one considered to be the Lord of one's life.

The Greek translation of the Hebrew word for the "Lord" (*Jahweh* or *Adonai*) was *Kyrios*. When Christians heard the word *Kyrios* in connection with the emperor they felt that a human was claiming to be God. It seemed to them that the emperor was attempting to compete with the lordship of Jesus Christ. The decision confronting them was whether they would belong to the *Kyrios* Domitian or to the *Kyrios* Jesus, the Christ. When they were asked simply to burn a few kernels of incense on the charcoal altar in tribute to the emperor, they must have been sorely tempted. A person could thus buy his life and freedom, and nobody cared what else he did. But the Christian had to say No. He would obey the law of the land, pay taxes, respect the emperor and other authorities, he would do whatever else the state required (Romans 13:1–7; I Peter 2:13–17), but he could not worship the emperor. Christians gave their blood and their lives, which could have been saved simply by the act of burning the incense for the emperor. The book of Revelation addresses itself to this situation.

With this background of information we can understand the meaning of some of the words and the imagery that appear in the book. The beast (13:1 ff.; 17:3 ff.), the dragon (12:3 ff.), and the whore of Babylon (17:1 ff.) are all code references to the Roman empire and emperors and their demonic character. Those men, women, and children who were experiencing the first real persecution of the Christian faith would hear and understand ("If any one has an ear, let him hear" 13:9).

Many artists have portrayed the imagery of the book of the Revelation. One scene follows another in rapid succession. We see the heavenly throne with twenty-four other thrones surrounding it (chapter 4). We see the mysterious book with the seven seals, and the Lamb which alone can break the seals (chapter 5). We see the four apocalyptic horsemen (6:1–8), recognize the mysteries under the altar (6:9–11), experience the shaking of the whole structure of the universe as a new Israel is established (6:12–7:7), and we hear the silence when the seventh seal is opened (8:1).

Already we notice how the book utilizes the number seven as a number of sacred design. Here again, reference is made to the first creation. The book of Revelation mirrors the first creation; in new steps of seven, a new world will come into being.

After the seven seals have been broken open we hear of seven trumpets (8:2). Each one is sounded, and with each new blast signaling a new catastrophe, some dire event occurs on land or sea, sun, moon, or stars (8:6–10:7). John is now instructed to do something strange, something the prophet Ezekiel once did also (Ezekiel 2:8–3:3). He is told to eat a small scroll given him by the angel. In his mouth it tasted sweet as honey, but in his stomach it turned very bitter (10:8–10). It is sweet to take in the word of God, but terribly bitter to be the prophet of the great judgment (10:11).

The third group of seven is the vision of the seven bowls of wrath (chapters 15–16), which we recognize from the paintings of the great masters as the bowls containing terrible plagues that would be poured out over the earth.

These scenes are merely preludes to the final victory of the Christ. Judgment of the world is pronounced (chapters 18–20), and then the heavenly Jerusalem is seen coming down from heaven to complete God's plan for his creation (chapters 21–22). In these concluding chapters of the book the beauty of the new creation is unveiled. The most striking feature of this new Jerusalem, as John tells it, is this:

> And I saw no temple in the city, for its temple is the Lord God the Almighty and the Lamb. And the city has no need of sun or moon to shine upon it, for the glory of God is its light, and its lamp is the Lamb. By its light shall the nation walk. . . .
>
> REVELATION 21:22–24

Because the Lord himself will dwell in the midst of His people, there will be no need for a temple. He will dwell among them as a father among his children, and as a friend among friends. This vision pictures the restoration of a world and of men who had lost their harmony and intimate relationship with God in the fall, as told in the book of Genesis.

In the center of this great panorama stands the scene of the battle of Michael and his angels with "the dragon, . . . that ancient serpent, who is called the Devil and Satan" (Revelation 12:9). A close look at this one scene, out of the dozens described in Revelation, will clarify some important points. When we read chapter 12 carefully, beginning with verse 7, and interpret carefully what we have read, we discover the following: the victory for which Michael and the other angels are to fight has, in fact, already been won. The sequence of seals and trumpets and bowls of wrath means, really, that the final outcome, the victory of the Lord over all evil, is not some future event. It is an accomplished fact for the faithful. Many have read into the book of Revelation uncertainty and fear, but the book is filled with hope, because the central message is: "Now the salvation and the power and the kingdom of our God and the authority of his Christ have come" (12:10). The victory of the angels—and the victory of the faithful, the martyrs and those who will be victims of persecution—is only a kind of aftermath; because the real victory has been won in the resurrection of Jesus Christ (1:5–7). The general of the angel armies, Michael, has a classical Hebrew name meaning, "Who is like God?" There *is* no one like God. Even the angels, including Michael, are creatures, as man is a creature, and in spite of all the horror of the world, it is God who is the master.

That is the significant note in this twelfth chapter and, indeed, in the entire book: "Woe to you, O earth and sea, for the devil has come down to you in great wrath, because he knows that his time is short!" (12:12). What John seemed to know, and what we must not forget, is that the Devil is already overcome, that his time is short and his reign limited.

At this point we see and feel how close Revelation is to the message of the prophets and seers of the old covenant in the Hebrew Bible. They too did not spare anyone. Their messages were brutal and cruel in their clarity. There was judgment and there was condemnation, but only as a structure within the grace of God, only to bring about the reign of God, His kingdom. To be fascinated by the overwhelming imagery of the book, to see only the bowls of wrath and hear only the ear-piercing trumpets of the day of judgment, to shudder at the scroll with the seven seals and to be terrified at the thought of what they might contain is to miss the message of the book.

It is the gift of the children of God to look at this world and to know that God rules. Those who know that the final outcome is God's can bear willingly what has to be borne, and they may even be able to do it with a lilt and a kind of holy smile. Without a book like the book of Revelation we might think that the future depends solely on us, and that we have to save ourselves. It is somewhat humbling to learn that God has already won the victory, and has graciously given us permission to do the mopping-up operations. To a careful reader the book of Revelation shows that men have a place in God's plan, but only as little soldiers, knowing that the battle is won, that Satan has only a little time left. Such faith faces the future with optimism.

Almost every age claims itself to be the worst ever. We like to think of ourselves as people who are enduring greater trials and facing greater dangers than any previous generation. Having read our way through the record of the Hebrew prophets, and having looked through the window opened by the book of Revelation, we know that each age has its own troubles and its own glories, its own nearness to God, its own form of remoteness from Him. There is no age that is "worse" and no age that is "better," because the really decisive consideration is whether one lives *with* God or *apart* from Him in isolation and rebellion. The distance Adam and Eve established between themselves and God, in their disobedience, remains, and characterizes each successive generation. The nearness established by God's love and grace is an ongoing reality. Whether an age seems to have the taste of peace, therefore, or overwhelms one with its troubles, each man in whatever era he lives has the opportunity to live with God. That hope, already present to the eyes of faith, is seen in its fulfillment in that glorious final vision of the book of Revelation: "And night shall be no more; they need no light of lamp or sun, for the Lord God will be their light" (22:5).